SLACKPACKING
THE
CAMINO
FRANCES

By
Sylvia Nilsen

Lightfoot Guide

'Slackpacking' is a relatively new term used to describe any kind of trekking or hiking with support. Whether trekking with pack-horses in the Andes, donkeys in Peru, or employing Sherpa when hiking in the Himalaya, slackpacking has been the preferred mode of trekking for millennia.

It is thought that the term was first used to describe hikers doing the Appalachian Trail in the US with backup support and resupply. In contrast to the extreme hikers who trek long distances carrying heavy loads on their backs and sleeping outdoors, the slackpacker carries a daypack with basic necessities and transfers the rest of his or her baggage ahead. On many such treks rooms in hostels or hotels are pre-booked.

Any tour company that offers multi-day walks with baggage transfer and accommodation booked, whether it is guided or guided, is offering a slackpacking experience."

Published in 2013 by Paul Chinn and Babette Gallard www.pilgrimagepublications.com
ISBN: 978-2-917183-28-1

Written by Sylvia Nilsen
www.sylvianilsenbooks.weebly.com

First edition, 2013
© Sylvia Nilsen 2013
© Sketches: Sandi Beukes 2012
© Front cover: "Cruz de Ferro" by Sylvia Nilsen
© Camino Lingo Accommodation: Reinette Novòa

About the author

Sylvia Nilsen is a South African freelance writer who has been published in numerous local and international publications. She worked as a research agent and editor for a UK-based travel guide publisher and produced several African city and country guides.

Sylvia has walked over 5 000 km of Camino trails in France and Spain, as well as from Switzerland to Rome on the Via Francigena pilgrimage.

She has served as a volunteer hospitalero in Spain and is a Spanish accredited hospitalero volunteer trainer in South Africa having trained 42 new volunteers.

With amaWalkers Camino (Pty) Ltd she leads small groups of pilgrims on slackpacking trails on the Camino Frances.

This is Sylvia's 7th pilgrimage related book.

Other books by this author published by LightFoot Guides

YOUR CAMINO on foot, bicycle or horseback in France and Spain

A comprehensive Camino planning guide offering advice to pilgrims on choosing a route, how to get to the start, info for people with disabilities, cyclists, walking with children, with a dog, a donkey or doing the Camino on horseback, with 300 pages of advice and information.

CAMINO LINGO, English-Spanish Words and Phrases for Pilgrims on el Camino de Santiago.
Compiled by Sylvia Nilsen and her Spanish teacher Reinette Novóa, this is a cheat's guide to speaking Spanish on the Camino. No complicated verb conjugations or rules on grammar, this book offers over 650 words and phrases just for pilgrims.

e-Books available from Amazon Kindle

- **Pilgrim Footprints on the Sands of Time**
  (12th century historical novel)

- **Three Short Hikes on el Camino de Santiago**
  (Aragones Route, Camino Ingles and Santiago to Finisterre plus 15-day hospitalera in San Roque)

- **La via Turonensis – from Paris to Spain**
  (1120km walk to Spain in the 2004 Holy Year)

- **La via Francigena – Five Pilgrims to Rome**
  (From Switzerland to Rome in 2006)

ACKNOWLEDGMENTS

Pilgrimage Publications:
I am especially grateful to Babette and Paul at Pilgrimage Publications for taking this book on as a project.

People who shared information from their websites include:

Joan Fiol – Gronze.com: Camino maps
Arturo Murias – Godesalco.com: Itineraries
Photos from Wikipedia
Reinette Novóa – for Appendix 1 from Camino Lingo
Sandi Beukes for the illustrations

Disclaimer
At the time of going to print, the distances between towns and villages were correct. Hotels, pensiones, hostales and other accommodation websites were checked as correct. Place names change, hotels close down and new ones open; websites, telephone numbers and email addresses change. Sometimes routes are changed and new deviations or detours are established which can affect the mileages.

Changes are inevitable and we welcome any feedback on changes that will enable us to enhance the quality of this guide. Please post changes or new information on my website:
www.sylvianilsensbooks.weebly.com

CONTENTS

Chapter 4

Chapter 5

Appendices

Appendix 1

Appendix 2

Appendix 3

Appendix 4

Appendix 5

Introduction

"I've walked to Santiago seven times since 2002, mostly carrying a full backpack and sleeping in pilgrim shelters. Every year the number of pilgrims grew and I started to dread the daily race for beds and queuing for a bunk-bed in over-crowded shelters. Staying in rooms, especially private pilgrim refuges, means that I still enjoy the camaraderie of other pilgrims, and get a good night's sleep! Being able to send my back-pack ahead some days also makes a huge difference to my enjoyment of walking the Camino. Just knowing that I have a bed and a hot shower waiting for me at the end of the day takes all the stress and anxiety out of walking. It gives me time to smell the wildflowers, stop for lunch or do some sight-seeing if I want to".
Sylvia Nilsen 2013

Pilgrims on the Camino – then and now

From the time the tomb of the apostle James the Greater was discovered in the 9th century, there has been a melting pot of people on the road to Santiago with as many different types of pilgrims in the Middle Ages as there are today. Besides the hoards of poor, unemployed and penitential pilgrims foot-slogging thousands of miles to the tomb of the apostle, we read about lords and ladies with their entourages, kings and queens with their servants and slaves (who might have carried the lords and ladies in litters for much of the way!); ecclesiastic pilgrims – priests, bishops and even a couple of popes - accompanied by their servants and clerics, and knights travelling with their ladies with their large retinues. These pilgrims would have been hosted in the best monastic quarters, the finest inns, or in castles and palaces with the local royalty.

Many pilgrims went on horseback; others had donkeys or mules to bear their loads. Most of the classic pilgrim stories that have come down to us were written by pilgrims on horseback. There are historical accounts of large caravans of pilgrims on the roads to Santiago – some with camels!

The majority of pilgrims did not walk alone but walked in groups for safety sake. In many countries, large towns and cities had guilds that organised guided group walks to Santiago. It was much safer to travel this way and, like the tour groups of today, pilgrims walked with like-minded people and supported each other on the long journey.

St Bona of Pisa, patron saint of travelers and specifically pilgrims, guides, couriers and flight attendants, led ten such groups of pilgrims from Italy to Santiago in the 12th century and was made an official pilgrim guide by the Knights of Santiago.

From the end of the 15th century, anyone who could afford to was able to travel with the postal service – a service with horses and carts that were changed at regular staging posts. From the mid-17th century the 'Grand Tour' became popular and it was possible to travel in comfort with a 'Cicerone' (a knowledgeable tour guide) and travel agents known as 'carters' provided transport, accommodation and food on the road to Santiago.

Slackpacking might be a new term but has been a popular way to trek since the beginning of time and having someone cart your luggage each day while you hike a trail is nothing new. It is becoming more and more popular as people who are not normally extreme hikers take to the trails around the world.

Pilgrimage has always had a commercial aspect with taxes collected to maintain roads and bridges, vendors providing goods and souvenirs, locals offering rooms and tour guides offering safe passage to groups. The large pilgrim churches along the pilgrimage routes in France and Spain survived mainly on donations and bequests made by pilgrims.

Doing "The Way" your way

Everyone is entitled to do the Camino their way. Some pilgrims like to walk alone, carrying everything they posses on their backs and staying only in pilgrim shelters. Others enjoy walking for long distances, starting in different countries and taking many months to walk to Santiago – often camping along the way.

Until the reanimation of the old pilgrimage trails in the late 1970s nearly every pilgrim to Santiago arrived there by bus or train. Many went with organised groups or tours, as they still do to other Christian shrines such as Jerusalem, Rome and Fatima or Lourdes. Very few people walk to these shrines.

Over 10 million pilgrims visited Santiago in 2010 (a Holy Year) and of those, only 2% (272 700) walked or cycled the route, the bulk covering the last 100 km. The great majority arrived there by plane, car, bus and train.

Perhaps you prefer not to walk alone for weeks carrying everything on your back, or rough it by staying in crowded pilgrim hostels.

You can choose to walk alone and take pot-luck on finding a room when you arrive in a village or town. (Look out for signs that advertise "Habitaciones/ Rooms/ Zimmer/ Chambre.) Just remember, if you don't have a place booked you will have to carry your backpack.

You can book your accommodation ahead of time and have your backpack transferred each day. Or you might prefer to walk with like-minded people in an organized group. You can book guided and unguided tours on the Camino with any of the reputable companies listed in this book. If you are pressed for time you can choose to walk a section of the trail, then get a bus or taxi further down the route. Many people don't have five or six weeks to spare, meaning that they have to take a taxi or a bus to a few places.

This book is to help you plan your perfect Camino. It can be used alone or as a companion to my comprehensive planning guide "YOUR CAMINO on foot, bicycle or horseback in France and Spain".

Is this book for you?

- *You want to do the Camino but don't fancy staying in crowded dormitories or pilgrim refuges every night.*

- *You would you prefer to take your time walking, stopping when you want to and sightseeing, knowing that you have a room with a hot shower waiting for you at the end of the day.*

- *You would prefer to carry just a day-pack and send your heavier baggage ahead where possible.*

- *You can afford to pay upwards of €18 per day for a private room and between €5 and €7 per day to have your luggage transferred.*

If you said YES to these five statements, then this is the perfect book to plan your Camino!

Chapter 1

WHEN AND WHERE TO START WALKING

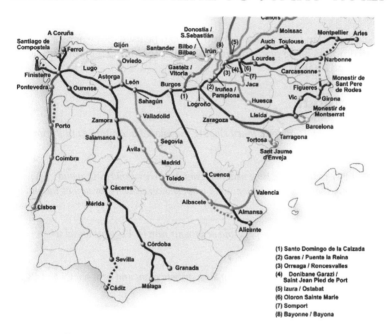

(1) Santo Domingo de la Calzada
(2) Gares / Puente la Reina
(3) Orreaga / Roncesvalles
(4) Donibane Garazi /
    Saint Jean Pied de Port
(5) Izura / Ostabat
(6) Oloron Sainte Marie
(7) Somport
(8) Bayonne / Bayona

In Spain, 'all roads lead to Santiago'. This book focuses on one road, the **Camino Frances**, the route most people have read about, or seen a film on it. This is the Jacobean Route par excellence, the one with the best infrastructures, buses, trains, transport companies, airports, and the largest variety of accommodations.

Many guide books list the starting place for the Camino Frances at the medieval village of St Jean Pied de Port (St John at the Foot of the Pass) in France, or at Roncesvalles in the Spanish Pyrenees.

In the Middle Ages pilgrims left from their front door which might have been 1000 km or 120 km from Santiago! You can start walking this route from anywhere along the 780km trail – including St Jean and Roncesvalles - but also from Pamplona, Burgos, Leon, O Cebreiro or Sarria.

If you want to earn the Compostela, the certificate of completion based on a 14th century document, you will have to prove to the pilgrim's office staff that you have walked the last 100 km to Santiago by producing a pilgrims' passport (the Credencial) filled with stamps from the places where you have stayed or from tourist offices, churches, bars etc. The nearest biggish town to the 100 km mark is Sarria -114 km from Santiago.

Towns that are easily reached where you can start your Camino

St Jean Pied de Port	775 km (from Santiago)
Roncesvalles	750 km
Pamplona	707 km
Burgos	490 km
Leon	312 km
Astorga	266 km
Ponferrada	210 km
O Cebreiro	158 km
Sarria	114 km

Credencial del Peregrino – Pilgrims' Passport

The Credencial will give you access to the albergues in Spain, including the private albergues. You can obtain this passport from the St James association in your country or from the pilgrim's office in St Jean, the albergue in Roncesvalles or Pamplona. It is also available from some churches, cathedrals or tourism offices in Spain.

Although you are 'slackpacking' and staying in private rooms, the private albergues, where you can book ahead or have your luggage transferred to, require that you present the pilgrim's credential in order to stay with them. (You don't need one for other establishments.)

When you register at the albergue, you will receive a rubber stamp in your passport and these are often a wonderful souvenir of your pilgrimage with delightful stamps from all the different places you've stayed in.

You will need to present the stamped credencial at the Pilgrim's Office in Santiago in order to earn the Compostela, a certificate of completion given to all pilgrims who walk the last 100 km or cycle the last 200 km to Santiago.

BEST TIME TO WALK A CAMINO

The best months to walk the Camino Frances are May/June and September/October. Spring arrives late in the northern villages of Spain and in the Pyrenees there can be snowfalls and heavy rain right up to the end of April. Spring is a great time to walk, when everything is green, the wild-flowers are spectacular and the large white and black European stork all have fat babies in their huge nests on top of church towers and specially built towers.

In September the countryside is drier but although the stork and flowers have long gone, walking in autumn has its own beauty with fields of gold and ochre and the gifts of harvest time. The grapes are heavy on the vines, wild bramble berries line the paths, figs, nuts, raspberries and other fruits are plentiful.

July and August are generally hot months and, with August being the Spanish holiday month, the trails and pilgrim accommodation in Spain can become overcrowded.

By the end of October the chill returns and it can be frosty in the high places in October and November. Daylight hours are shortened and whilst the sun sets after 10pm in May and June, sunrise in October is 8am and sunset before 7pm.

Winter is the most challenging time to walk, with even shorter daylight hours, probability of heavy snowfalls covering the yellow arrows and many places closed.

Weather Tables

These weather tables detail 30-year average weather figures on the Camino Frances.

MAY

	Daily temp	Av max temp	Av min temp	Rain-fall	Rainy Days
Pamplona	14.0	19.8	8.2	74	10
Logroño	15.3	21.0	9.5	48	8
Burgos	11.4	17.2	5.6	69	10
León	12.1	18.0	6.2	58	9
Ponferrada	14.4	20.4	8.5	59	10
Santiago	12.9	17.7	8.1	147	14

JUNE

	Daily temp	Av max temp	Av min temp	Rain-fall	Rainy Days
Pamplona	17.5	23.9	11.2	47	6
Logroño	19.0	25.4	12.6	47	5
Burgos	15.2	22.0	8.4	46	6
León	16.4	23.2	9.5	39	6
Ponferrada	18.6	25.4	11.8	34	6
Santiago	16.0	21.3	10.7	82	8

	Daily temp	Av max temp	Av min temp	Rain-fall	Rainy Days
Pamplona	18.0	24.4	11.7	43	6
Logroño	19.1	25.4	12.7	24	4
Burgos	15.7	22.9	8.5	36	5
León	16.4	22.9	9.9	39	4
Ponferrada	17.9	24.3	11.4	49	6
Santiago	17.0	22.3	11.7	127	9

OCTOBER

	Daily temp	Av max temp	Av min temp	Rain-fall	Rainy Days
Pamplona	13.6	18.7	8.4	74	8
Logroño	14.1	19.3	8.9	31	6
Burgos	10.9	16.5	5.3	50	8
León	11.4	16.4	6.4	56	8
Ponferrada	12.9	17.8	7.9	74	9
Santiago	13.4	17.7	9.1	194	13

WHERE TO START AND HOW TO GET THERE

Starting at St Jean - 775km

Getting to St Jean Pied de Port

UK to Bayonne
From London - Eurolines – National Express overnight coach.

Nearest airport Biarritz:
From the UK: Ryanair and EasyJet.

From Paris: If you fly to Paris, you can get a local flight or EasyJet flight to Biarritz. Or you can take a fast or slow train. www.sncf.com

There is no direct bus or train service to St Jean Pied de Port from the main cities of France or Spain. From France you have to get to Biarritz/Bayonne and then travel from there to St Jean by bus or train (whichever is running that day).

From Biarritz you can travel to Bayonne by train or on the #6 bus to the train station. It leaves about every 30 minutes and takes about 45 minutes. From Bayonne you take another train or bus to St Jean, about 1.5 hours through pretty countryside.
www.sncf.com

Download an up-to-date timetable here. Under 'My Journey' enter 'Line 62 Bayonne to St Jean Pied de Port' **http://tinyurl.com/bj9cmcu**
/
A quicker and easier way (but obviously more costly) is to take a taxi from Bayonne/ Biarritz to St Jean using the local taxi service: **www.taxisbiarritz.fr**

Express Bourricot (Smart Donkey), which is based in St Jean, operates a shuttle service between French airports and St Jean, transporting pilgrims from Pau, Bilbao and Irún to St Jean Pied de Port. There is a facility on their website to form a carpool. They also transport luggage over the mountain from St Jean to Roncesvalles.
www.expressbourricot.com

From Spain

From Madrid or Barcelona you can travel to Pamplona by train or bus. In Pamplona you have the choice of a daily, 18h00 bus to Roncesvalles where taxis wait to take pilgrims to St Jean. (No Sunday bus). **www.autocaresartieda.com**

In the summer, from mid-June to September, ALSA put on two buses a day between Pamplona and St Jean at 14h00 and 17h30, with one return bus at 19h30.
www.alsa (International search)

Or you can take the taxi from Pamplona to St Jean
Tel: 948 23 23 00   948 35 13 35

Weekdays: Pamplona to St Jean €96: Pamplona airport to St Pied €100.
Weekends and holidays: Pamplona to St Jean €120: Pamplona airport to St Jean €125.
There is an option to share a taxi with other pilgrims - more information on the website.
www.taxipamplona.com/comparte.php

Esprit du Chemin - a pilgrim hostel in St Jean - offers a page on their website for you to put your name down for a 'carpool' so that you can share a taxi to St Jean from Pamplona or Roncesvalles.
www.espritduchemin.org/EC/carpoolEN.html

They also have a link to the timetable for the rail/bus line to St Jean, a town map and information on parking your car in St Jean and walking the Camino from there.
www.espritduchemin.org/English/travelinfo.html

When you arrive in St Jean visit the Pilgrim's Office to collect a pilgrim passport (credencial) and your scallop shell, symbol of St James.
Accueil des pelerins de St-Jacques, 39 rue de la Citadelle. The office is open from 7h30 to 12h30 and then from 13h30 to 22h00.

Accommodation in St Jean Pied de Port
There is plentiful accommodation in St Jean from hiker's gîtes to B&Bs, pilgrim albergues and hotels. Use this handy website to find rooms by clicking on the accommodation logos on the interactive map. **http://tinyurl.com/adpgwg3**

Recommendations:

Budget: Gite Compostela
       http://gitecompostella.jimdo.com/
B&B: Errecaldia
       www.errecaldia.com/

Route Napoleon or through Val Carlos

There are two routes over the Pyrenean hills from St Jean to Roncesvalles. The 'road route' which is on the original pilgrim's route through the small village of Val Carlos (Valley of Charlemagne), now a small tarred road with many detours onto walking trails and paths, and a partly cross country route called the Route Napoleon which is a bit steeper and goes a bit higher than the route through Val Carlos.

On the Route Napoleon, many people take two days to walk from St Jean to Roncesvalles, stopping at Refuge Orisson which is 8km up from St Jean. The refuge only has 18 beds in a dormitory room and 6 two-person tents in the grounds behind the refuge. There are no private rooms in Orisson. If you don't mind sleeping in the tents, you can reserve one by emailing: **refuge.orisson@wanadoo.fr**

The better solution is to book rooms for two nights in St Jean. Walk to Orisson the next day, or beyond, and arrange for a local taxi to collect you from Orisson, or at the 11.5km mark where you will see the statue of the Biakorri Virgin on the rocks on your left.
The taxi can take you back to your accommodation in St Jean. The following day, the taxi can take you back to where you left off so that you can continue walking to Roncesvalles.

If walking two days on the road route you can stay at Val Carlos in a B&B or Casa Rural.
www.luzaide-valcarlos.net/es/fr_turismo.htm

Recommendations:

Hostal Maitena: **www.hostalmaitena.com**
Casa Marcelino: **www.casamarcelino.com**

Val Carlos Taxi: Ander Urolategui operates a taxi minivan for 8 people. Tours, hotel transfers, airport, train station. Mobile: 636 191 423. Tel / Fax: 948790218

Useful website: www.turismo.navarra.es

Starting at Roncesvalles - 750km

Getting to Roncesvalles

Nearest airport Pamplona

The airport is about 7 km from the city accessible by bus or taxi. The daily bus to Roncesvalles leaves from the main Pamplona bus station at 18h00 and takes 1 hour ten minutes to Roncesvalles. Monday to Friday: 18:00 (From July 1 to August 31 there is another at 10h00): Saturdays: 16:00 (July 1 to August 31, there is another at 10h00): Sundays: No Service: Price: €6
www.autocaresartieda.com/?scc=roncesvalles

From 1 June to September, the bus company ALSA.es has two buses per day at 14h00 and 17h30 from the Pamplona bus station to St Jean. It stops at Roncesvalles on the way €15. The return trip from St Jean is at 19:30. Tickets can be purchased online from the international section of ALSA

By Taxi

Teletaxi San Fermin Tel: 948 23 23 00   948 35 13 35
Weekdays: From Pamplona to Roncesvalles €57: from Pamplona airport to Roncesvalles €60
Weekends and holidays: From Pamplona to Roncesvalles €70: from Pamplona airport to Roncesvalles €75
There is an option to share a taxi with other pilgrims. More information
www.taxipamplona.com/comparte.php

Accommodation in Roncesvalles

Roncesvalles is a small monastery complex that boasts two inns, a new Hotel that occupies a part of the monastery and a pilgrims' hostel – where you can book a bunk bed. Your luggage will be transported to the La Posada.

Pilgrims' albergue	realcolegiata@hotmail.com
Casa de Beneficiados	www.casadebeneficados.com
La Posada	www.laposadaderoncesvalles.com
Casa Sabina	www.casasabina.es

Starting at Pamplona - 707km

Getting to Pamplona

Pamplona, the historical capital of Navarra, is famous for the San Fermin festival and the running of the bulls which takes place from 6 – 14 July every year. Accommodation in and around Pamplona is at a premium during the festival and prices quadruple.

From Madrid:
By bus: **www.alsa.es**
By train: **www.renfe.es**
Fly: **www.iberia.com**

From Barcelona:
By bus: **www.vibasa.es**
By train: **www.renfe.es**
There are three trains to Pamplona daily.

Accommodation in Pamplona

Check **Booking.com** for a variety of accommodation from pensiones and hostales to five star hotels.

Recommendations:

Pension Sarasate **http://pensionsarasate.es/**
Hotel la Perla   **www.granhotellaperla.com/**
(Ernest Hemingway's room has been preserved in this recently renovated 5-star hotel.)

Starting at Burgos – 490km

Getting to Burgos

From Barcelona
Train: **www.renfe.es**
Bus: **www.alsa.es**

From Madrid
Three trains a day: **www.renfe.es**
About 20 buses per day: **www.Alsa.es**

Accommodation in Burgos

Check Booking.com for a variety of accommodation from pensiones and hostales to five star hotels.

Recommendations

AC Hotel Burgos
www.marriott.com/hotels/travel/rgsbu-ac-hotel-burgos/
Hotel Maria Luisa
www.marialuisahotel.com/es/burgos/

Starting at Leon – 312km

Getting to Leon

From Barcelona
By bus: **www.alsa.es**

By train: **www.renfe.es**

From Bilbao
By train: **www.renfe.es**

From Madrid
By bus: **www.alsa.es**
By train: **www.renfe.es**
By air: Fly to Valladolid.
Alsa.es runs a direct bus service from the airport to Leon – 1h45mins.

Accommodation in Leon

Check **Booking.com** for a variety of accommodation from pensiones and hostales to five star hotels and a parador.

Recommendations

Hostal San Martín   **www.sanmartinhostales.es/**
Hotel Albany   **www.albanyleon.com**
Parador de Leon   **www.parador.es/en/parador-de-leon**

Getting to Astorga

By bus: There are 4 daytime buses from Madrid to Astorga

Or From Madrid to Leon:

Travel to Leon by train or bus. You can get the ALSA bus from Madrid Barajas airport. It takes about five hours **www.alsa.es**

Train: **www.renfe.es**
The train station you need is Madrid-Chamartin. You get there on the metro line which leaves from the airport.

Once in Leon you can get an ALSA bus to Astorga. There are over 20 buses a day, they take about 50 minutes

Accommodation in Astorga

Check **Booking.com** for a variety of accommodation from pensiones and hostales to five star hotels

Recommendations

Hotel Gaudi   **www.gaudihotel.es**
Hostal Coruña   **www.reservascoruna.net/**

Getting to Ponferrada

From Bilbao
By bus: **www.alsa.es**
By train: **www.renfe.es**

From Madrid:
By bus: **www.alsa.es**
By train: **www.renfe.es**

Accommodation in Ponferrada

Check Booking.com for a variety of accommodation from pensiones and hostales to five star hotels.

Recommendations

Hotel Los Templarios   **www.hotellostemplarios.info**
Aroi Ponferrada   **www.aroihoteles.com**
Hotel Novo   **www.hotelnovo.com/es/index.html**

Getting to O Cebreiro

There is no public transport to the hilltop village of O Cebreiro. Buses stop at Piedrafita Cebreiro which is at the bottom of the hill, about 5km from O Cebreiro. You can walk up the tarred road to O Cebreiro, a pleasant 5km walk with picnic tables on the side of the road about half-way up. Or, you can take a taxi from Piedrafita to O Cebreiro.

From Bilbao
By bus to Piedrafita: **www.alsa.es**

From Madrid
By bus to Piedrafita: **www.alsa.es**

From Pamplona
By bus to Piedrafita via Lugo **www.alsa.es**

From Santiago de Compostela
By bus to Piedrafita **www.alsa.es**

Accommodation in O Cebreiro

There are more inns and Casas in O Cebreiro than local homes! Check the Spain info website for a complete list and reserve a room from there.
http://tinyurl.com/b6trjmy

Recommendations

Hostal Residencia San Giraldo de Aurillac
Casa Rural Venta Celta*
Casa Rural Centro de Turismo Rural Casa Carolo

Getting to Sarria

From Madrid:
By Train: Monday to Friday and Sunday (no service on Saturday): There is a Hotel-Train at 22:30 which arrives in Sarria at 6:50 the next day. **www.renfe.es**

From Santiago:
You can fly to Santiago and take a taxi from there or a bus to Lugo and from there to Sarria.

Flights to Santiago:
There are 5 daily flights on Iberia, from Madrid to Santiago (1hr10mins) ± $134 return (€101) or check RyanAir for flights 'in season' for about $40 (€30) one way

By bus from Santiago (you will need to take two buses – one to Lugo and then to Sarria)

To Lugo: The Company Freire, SL runs between Santiago and Lugo. You can get the bus from the Santiago airport or from the bus station in Santiago. Check the timetables on the website **http://www.empresafreire.com**

From Lugo to Sarria: The Company Monforte, SA runs buses from Lugo to Sarria. There are several buses every day of the week. **http://www.monbus.es**

Taxi: From Santiago airport to Sarria for about $132 (€100). The taxis take 4 people so you could share with other pilgrims

Accommodation in Sarria

Check **Booking.com** for a variety of accommodation from pensiones and hostales to five star hotels.

Recommendations

Casa Matias	Booking.com
Pension/apartment Escalanata	www.pensionescalinata.es
Hotel Oca Villa de Sarria	Booking.com

Getting back home

- The Central Bus Station in Santiago is at Plaza Camilo Díaz Baliño: Tel: 54 981 24 1 **www.tussa.org.**
- The Train Station – Rua Hórreo: Tel: 902 240 202 **www.renfe.es**
- The Freire bus line connects Santiago to Lavacolla airport. Tel: 58 981 81 11 **www.empresafreire.com**
- La Coruna: You can go by bus or train: **www.renfe.es** Bus is cheaper and more frequent. **www.monbus.es**
- Barcelona: Fly Spanair, Vueling or Ryanair. By bus 17 hours – no direct train.
- Biarritz: Train **www.renfe.es**
- Bilbao: Train **www.renfe.es** 10.5 hours
- Irun: Train **www.renfe.es** 11.5 hours
- Madrid: Iberia and Ryanair fly to Madrid. Train **www.renfe.es** Bus: **www.alsa.es**
- Paris: You can take the Renfe train from Santiago which leaves about 9h00 and connects with the SNCF night train at Hendaye arriving in Paris at about 7h00, or fly on **Vueling.com**

Airlines that fly from Santiago's Lavacolla airport

Aerolineas Argentinas	Buenos Aires-Ezeiza
Aer Lingus	Dublin [seasonal]
Air Berlin	Palma de Mallorca
Air Europa	Fuerteventura, Lanzarote,
	Las Palmas de Gran Canaria, Tenerife-South
Iberia	Madrid

Ryanair (seasonal so check website **ryanair.com**)

Chapter 2

ACCOMMODATION

There are many different types of accommodation on the Camino Frances with something to satisfy every pilgrim from basic rooms in private pilgrim refuges to sumptuous suites in paradores.

Different types of accommodation

Parador *(Photo Wiki)*

Paradores are top class luxury hotels in monasteries, castles, palaces and other historic buildings. Guests between 20 and 35 years of age (inclusive) can often stay at participating paradores for under €60 per person per night with buffet breakfast included. During low season, guests 55 years and older can enjoy a 30% discount.

The Hostal de los Reyes Catolicos in Santiago was built in 1499 as a pilgrim hospice and hospital. It became a hotel in 1953 and is one of Spain's most sumptuous state run paradores with rooms costing from €210 to €525 per night. It retains the tradition of providing a free meal to at least ten pilgrims each day.   Some paradores offer a limited number of double/twin standard rooms from €60 per night and reduced rates for seniors. Rooms must be booked in advance. **www.paradores-spain.com**

Hotel

One to five-star hotels can be found throughout Spain. Most hotels have seasonal price structures and room charges will depend on the time of year you travel. The annual Guía oficial de hotels published by the Instituto de Turismo de España is available from most bookstores, or contact your local Spanish Tourist Board for a copy.
www.spainbookers.com/

Casa rural

These country houses include B&B, cottages and apartments. Accommodation ranges from simple and homely to upmarket luxury. **www.coloursofspain.com**

Posada

A chain of affiliated lodging inns or rustic hotels (not to be confused with fondas), these are usually upmarket country or city inns with good accommodation and meals.
www.posadascaminodesantiago.com/alojamientos.php

Hostal

A little downscale from hotels – the hostales are graded according to a three-star system. (Not to be confused with hostels). **www.todohotel.com/Hoteles/hostales.html**

Pension

Marked with a 'P' on a sign, there are many more pensiones than fondas and they generally offer more up-market accommodation than the fondas. Many are family owned and in towns and cities occupy one or two floors in a general purpose building.

Fonda

Marked with a white 'F' on a blue sign, the fondas are small inns; most are very basic and do not offer en suite bathrooms or any luxuries.

Hostels

Spain has about 200 youth hostels, most of which are members of the Red Española de Albergues Juveniles (REAJ). (Not to be confused with the hostales) **www.reaj.com**

Albergue del peregrinos

Albergues are also known as refugios, refuges, pilgrim shelters and albergues del peregrinos.

In 1987, at a meeting of interested Camino Associations in Jaca, it was decided to create special overnight lodgings along the Camino Frances for pilgrims. Each region was responsible for motivating for the church and municipality to provide 'refuges' for pilgrims – not for tourists – in their area. Found in almost every town and village, they follow a 1 000-year-old tradition of providing shelter to pilgrims on their way to the tomb of St James.

In order to differentiate between tourist and pilgrim, a simple 'credencial' or pilgrim's passport was designed. These are carried by the pilgrim and produced at the 'refugios', churches, museums, tourist offices etc along the way where they are stamped to prove that the pilgrim is walking, horse riding or cycling the Camino. The Spanish Federation of Hospitaleros Voluntarios (volunteer wardens) trains people to serve as volunteers in the many donativo pilgrim shelters in Spain. Training courses can also be done in the USA, Canada, South Africa, France and Italy.

On the Camino Frances there are 10 645 beds spread over 242 hostels. The average price for a bunk bed in a hostel is €6.50. There is, on average, a place with a shelter every 6.3 km. Pilgrim refuges are found in restored churches, halls, renovated barns, private homes and specially built structures. Some are open all year; others only in summer, so always check your guide book before deciding on where to stay.

What are they like?

Some are modern and upmarket, others are ancient and basic. Some are small and accommodate only 10 or 12 people. (Medieval shelters often housed 12 pilgrims, the number of the apostles.) Others can accommodate 200 people.

In Hospital de San Nicolas, 10 people sleep in the loft of a restored hermitage church. As part of the pilgrim blessing the hospitaleros wash the pilgrim's feet – following the tradition of Maundy Thursday when Christ washed the feet of his disciples – and you have a communal dinner by lamplight.

Some of the 242 albergues on the Camino Frances are up-market, like university campus digs with all mod-cons including vending machines, cafeteria, bar and computer room with Internet. Many also have wifi.

Some albergues are supported by the church, some by the local government or municipality; others are owned and run by volunteers from different Confraternities of St James around the world. There are albergues that are owned by individuals or families who have devoted their lives to providing shelter to pilgrims. Most of the municipal, church and confraternity owned albergues are 'donativo' – for a donation. The municipal or church sponsored albergues in the Province of Galicia charge €6.

You cannot book a bed ahead at a donativo church, municipal or CSJ owned albergue. These are run on a first come, first served basis. Most of these also don't accept pilgrims with vehicle back-up, those who have sent their backpacks on ahead, or who have arrived by bus, train or taxi, and many do not accept large groups – usually more than six pilgrims. These albergues also have a 'pecking order' in that walking pilgrims take priority and pilgrims on bicycles often have to wait until evening before being told whether or not they have a bed for the night.

Some of the newer albergues offer private single and double rooms, rooms for four or six people with en suite bathroom and dormitories that sleep up to 80 pilgrims. The charges vary from €5 for a general dormitory to €30 for a private double room. Many of the privately owned albergues have come together under the umbrella of an organisation called Red de Albergues Camino de Santiago. They publish an annually updated fold-out list of all the albergues along the Camino Frances, 'donde el Camino se hace reposo' (where the Camino sleeps), with the mileage between villages and towns, and symbols indicating whether the establishment has Internet, a kitchen, laundry facilities, a bar or restaurant, etc.

Their 'Rules of Use' are that the albergues are for the exclusive use of pilgrims on foot, bicycle or horseback who have the pilgrims' credential. However, one can reserve beds ahead at many of these albergues and they also provide contact details for pilgrims wanting to send their backpacks on ahead.

If you would like to experience the camaraderie of staying in an albergue and interacting with other pilgrims, without having to sleep in overcrowded dormitories, these types of albergues are the ideal option. You will sleep in a private room but will share the public areas, kitchen and/or dining room with pilgrims from all over the world. **www.redalberguessantiago.com**

To find out more about the pilgrim albergues you can visit these websites:

Albergues in Spain:
www.caminodesantiago.consumer.es/

Accommodation in France:
www.chemindecompostelle.com/

Reserving rooms online

Booking hotel rooms

Internet booking

Booking accommodation over the internet has never been easier. You can book rooms directly with the hotel or use an online, hotel booking service.

You don't even need to be able to speak Spanish to book rooms. Most hotels will use a translator to translate your email request.

See Appendix 1 for a list of Spanish words and phrases to help you make reservations online in Spanish. (Taken from the book 'CAMINO LINGO English-Spanish Words and Phrases for Pilgrims on el Camino de Santiago')

Most accommodation booking websites like Booking.com are paid a commission by the hotel so you are not charged upfront for the reservation. In many cases you don't pay for the rooms until you arrive there. They will take your credit card details and if you do not pitch up, they will charge the booking to your card. Some charge a small deposit which is refundable up to a certain cut-off date.

Which Internet booking service to use?

Frommer's recently did a survey in search of the best and the not-so-best hotel booking websites taking into consideration the ease in making the reservation, how much information about each hotel is given, if customer reviews are provided, what fees are charged and best of all, if it truly is a rock-bottom deal. Read more here: http://tinyurl.com/aplcm4l

Frommers' top six hotel booking sites

Booking.com
Hotels.com
morehotels4less.com
Getaroom.com
Hotelreservations.com
HotelGuide.com

Booking rooms in Hostels

Many hostels have private rooms some with shared bathrooms, that are excellent value.

Read reviews on the top hostel booking websites by TravelChimps here:
http://inblighty.com/best-hostel-booking-sites.php

TravelChimps top six hostel booking sites

Hostelbookers.com
Hotelworld.com
Hihostels.com
Hostelz.com
Hostels.com
Hostelclub.com

Top Tour of Spain

This website provides a link to inns, hostels, pensions, hotels, paradores, monasteries and apartments, which they believe offer the best rates going.

www.top-tour-of-spain.com/hotel-information-for-spain.html/

www.top-tour-of-spain.com/Camino-de-Santiago-walking-tours.html

Chapter 3

LUGGAGE TRANSFERS AND CAMINO TOUR COMPANIES

Luggage Transfers

Many historical books, movies and websites on the Camino show statues, sculptures, stained glass windows and other works of art depicting pilgrims from the early 12th century to around the 18th century.

The majority of foot pilgrims wore a long, dark robe, carried a simple a shoulder bag called a 'scrip', a gourd for water and a staff.

Pilgrims who could afford it went on horseback and they were able to take extra changes in clothing and a few other comforts.

Backpacks

The one thing you won't see in books or film are medieval pilgrims carrying a backpack! A pilgrim from the middle ages would be astonished to see today's pilgrims slogging across the Camino with huge packs on their backs.

But, those were different times and modern pilgrims are expected to bathe and change and wash their clothes so most pilgrims carry extra clothing, washing soaps and toiletries and need a back-pack to carry their gear.

Most walking Camino pilgrims only need a small capacity pack to carry their clothing, medication and toiletries. If you intend sending your backpack ahead you could manage with a day-pack whilst walking but ensure that it is comfortable and secure.

In your pack you will carry a rain jacket or poncho, a jacket or fleece, a sitting plastic in case you decide to picnic on the side of the path or sit on a mossy wall, your first aid kit, snacks and drinks. I also recommend carrying your sandals so that you can change into them when you arrive at your hotel.

It is better to use a regular backpack, with padded shoulder straps, sternum strap and waist belt rather than a flimsy day pack with thin straps and no support that will swing around on your back as you go up and down hills.

If you do not want to carry a heavy backpack every day – or are unable to walk long distances over difficult terrain – you can still do the Camino by having your pack (and yourself) transported by taxi or transport services on most of the Camino routes. Remember, you only need to walk the last 100 km to Santiago to earn the Compostela certificate, and the pilgrims' office doesn't care how your backpack arrives there! (See Appendix 2 for packing lists)

In order to transfer luggage, you must have pre-booked accommodation along the way. This means that you will not be allowed to stay in the traditional 'donation' pilgrim albergues that do not allow pre-booking or vehicle back-up.
However, many private albergues do allow pilgrims to book rooms and have their backpacks transported along the route. Have a look at the private albergues lists here: **www.redalberguessantiago.com/documents/211.html**

Hotels usually have contact details of local taxis and luggage transfer service. Charges are from €7 per bag per stage. The bag should not weigh more than 12kg and a stage is up to 25km. The cost is half of that in Galicia (€3) where the number of pilgrims is much higher.

If you are walking with buddy or in a group, you can share a large shopping bag to send your excess stuff ahead. This helps to keep down the cost.

How does it work?

If you have all your accommodation pre-booked, you can arrange directly with the transfer company to transfer your bag every day. You'll send them an itinerary of dates and places and they will do the transfers every day.

If you only pre-book your accommodation a day or two ahead of time, you or your hotel must contact the transfer company the night before.

You might be asked to pay the hotel or you'll be given an envelope to put your money in. Write your name and the next place (or places) where you will be staying. Your bag must be in the lobby before 8am. The transfer company collects all the bags and delivers them to the different places – usually before 2pm.

Companies that transfer luggage

France

St Jean to Roncesvalles:
Express Bourricot provides shuttles from/to the airports at Biarritz, Pau and Toulouse to St Jean Pied de Port.
They will transport people from St Jean Pied de Port to Moissac (ex: Ostabat, Navarrenx, Aire sur l'Adour, Condom, Lectoure, etc). They also transport bags from St Jean to Roncesvalles. **www.expressbourricot.com**

Spain

Aragones Route

taxijavi@yahoo.es
Jaca, Huesca Tel: 637 503 920

Camino del Norte

Le P'tit Bag - transports bags from Irun to Bilbao.
g.car.trans@gmail.com
The Peregrine Express: Between Irún and Santander. If you are travelling in a big group and you have a minimum of 12 bags for transport they can transport as far as Oviedo. For information on transport past Oviedo: Tel: 644589217
christel.langeveld@gmail.com
http://theperegrineexpress.blogspot.com

Camino Frances

Caminofacil: From Roncesvalles to Santiago – bags and people, competitive prices.
www.caminofacil.net

Jacotrans: From St Jean Pied de Port to Santiago – bags and people. The site is in English, Spanish and French.
www.jacotrans.es Jacotrans@jacotrans.com

Toni Transport: Logroño: Pamplona to Burgos
Luggage Transportation and Pilgrims Services
Toni Transporte Tel: 636 099 299
http://toni-transporte.webcindario.com
Toni.transporte@gmail.com

Taxi Belorado:
From Roncesvalles to Santiago:
Javier Rioja Sáez: Tel: 947585002   610798138
www.taxibelorado.com   contacto@taxibelorado.com

Globetrotter Transportes: Transport of rucksacks, bicycles, etc. from Viana to Burgos from April to September: Transport luggage €7 per stage.   Tel: 667 386 387
www.chemindecompostelle.com/globetrotter/index.html

Luis Angel Acero: Burgos to Léon:
Tel: 650 451 540
www.taxiluisangel.com   Luisacero2005@yahoo.es

Taxi Sahagun: Castrojeriz to Léon
Tel: 659 563 390 689 399 556
www.taxisahagun.com/english.html
mavi46@gmail.com

Albergue Fenix: Léon to Villafranca del Bierzo and
O Cebreio. Villafranca to Travadelo, Ruitelan, Herrerias, La Faba and O Cebreiro. Public transport of bags and pilgrims
www.albergueavefenix.com info@albergueavefenix.com

Marimar Transportes: Taxi Astorga, Léon and Ponferrada
Marimar Gonzalez: **marimartransports@hotmail.com**

Camino de Santiago 2010: León to Santiago
Tel: 606049858 José Luis Pardo Rodriguez
www.Caminodesantiago2010.com.es
Info@Caminodesantiago2010.com.es

Xacotrans: Sarria to Santiago
They have more than fifty points for collection/delivery from Sarria, Portomarín, Palas de Rei, Melide, Arzúa,
O Pino, Lavacolla and Santiago. Including Disabled transport.
www.xacotrans.com
info@xacotrans.com

Embajada del peregrino: Palais de Rei to Santiago
They will deliver luggage in boxes from Palas de Rei to Melide, Arzua O Pino and Santiago de Compostela.
www.embajadadelperegrino.com/sintesis.htm

Via de la Plata

Taxi3 Amoeira: From Ourense:
Contact José Angel Cid Vazquez on: 629 035 774
You can use Taxi3 or other companies to start south of Ourense as well.
jacidvazquez@gmail.com

Posting luggage ahead

If you have extra luggage to continue your holiday after walking the Camino, or you find that you have packed too much stuff, you can post packages up to 20 kg ahead to yourself to any post office (Correos) in Spain and they will keep it for two weeks.

Postal addresses in Spain

Lista de Correos (Poste Restante)

31080 Pamplona
31100 Puenta la Reina
26080 Logroño
09080 Burgos
24080 León
24700 Astorga
2 4400 Ponferrada
27600 Sarria
15780 Santiago de Compostela (A Coruña)

Purchase a box at any post office (they are accustomed to sending on 'paquete peregrinos'). When sending your parcel to a post office, address the box as displayed. You will have to show your passport or ID when you collect it so write your name as it appears in your passport.

```
Your name
Lista de Correos
15780 Santiago de Compostela
La Coruña
```

If you are going to be on the Camino for longer than two weeks, you can post it to Ivar Revke who provides a storage facility in Santiago where it will be kept for up to 60 days for a small fee.

Open from Easter until the end of October – Mon to Fri: 10am to 2pm and on Saturday and Sunday by arrangement.

```
Ivar Rekve
ATT: Your Name
Travesia de la Universidade 1
15704 Santiago de Compostela
La Coruña, Spain
```

In the off season, send Ivar an email to make arrangements to collect your parcel. **ivar.rekve@gmail.com**

Small box (317 x 215 x 125 mm) €15 for 60 days
Medium box (390 x 290 x 190mm) €20 for 60 days
Large box (590 x 390 x 390mm) €25 for 60 days

Camino Tour Companies

There are many Camino tour companies that offer guided or unguided walks on the Camino. You can book guided or unguided walks for a few days to a few weeks with any of the reputable companies listed below.

amaWalkers Camino offer their "Best of Both, no-frills, accompanied 22-day walk for small groups (maximum 12) on the three most scenic sections of the Camino Frances in Spring and Fall . Their walks are called the 'Best of Both' because pilgrims don't only stay in comfortable hotels, inns and pensiones but also in a few private rooms in pilgrim albergues - no dormitories. This gives their groups an opportunity to interact with others walking the road and experience the camaraderie of sharing meals with pilgrims from all over the world. Walkers are free to walk at their own pace, or with the group leader, meeting up in the evening to share experiences. Luggage transfers and optional excursions are available.

www.amawalkerscamino.com
amawalkerscamino@gmail.com

Spanish Adventures

Garry lives in Santiago de Compostela and has been working as a guide on the Camino since early 2003. As well as guided trips, he offers self-guided trips on the Camino Frances, Camino Portuguese, Camino del Norte, Via de la Plata, Finisterre and the Camino Ingles. He will organise your accommodation (with dinners usually provided in the smaller towns) and bag transfers so you only need to carry a small day pack. He supplies labels for your bags each day to ensure your bags arrive at your accommodation. Stages are worked out according to your requirements and experience, and accommodation is selected according to your budget, in general using good quality local accommodation. He provides maps and suggestions on accommodation. He provides maps and suggestions on places for lunches and coffee breaks.

www.spanishadventures.com
garry@spanishadventures.com

Follow the Camino, Leading the Way since 2006

Become a part of the Camino family, enjoy the vibrant local culture, experience the ultimate inspirational inner journey; with Follow the Camino, you will love the Camino! Follow The Camino specialise in customising your Camino holidays along the legendary Camino de Santiago de Compostela. Our highly experienced consultants will design the incredible journey you always wanted; be it on the French Way, the Portuguese Way, Via de la Plata, Le Puy route, etc.

On foot, by bicycle, on horseback, or even by boat! we guarantee you an amazing experience every time; carrying your luggage along the Camino to make it a more inspiring trip, booking the best accommodation available to keep your mind at peace and catering for your more earthly needs (local authentic food, special dinners, etc.). Just tell us how you want it; we will make it for you.

Check out our website for special packages like the honeymoon Camino Romantico!
www.followthecamino.com
Find our unique Luggage Transfer Application:
https://followthecamino.com/community/luggage-transfers/
Find our Free App on I-store or Android: Camino Guide
Subscribe to our fun and informative newsletter: Camino News
www.followthecamino.com/en/newsletter/

The Camino Travel Centre

A local travel agent from Santiago de Compostela specialising in the Camino de Santiago. We help individual pilgrims and small groups. We offer: accommodation booking (private inns), luggage transfer, private transfer to the starting point of the Camino (taxi, bus), glass of wine with us upon the arrival to Santiago.
www.caminotravelcentre.com
contact@caminotravelcenter.com

Spanish Steps has been leading small group walking tours to Santiago for nearly 20 years. They offer trips along the Chemin de St. Jacques in France, the Camino Frances in Spain, the Camino del Norte, the Camino Primitivo and along the pilgrimage road to Rome known as the Via Francigena. These tours are fully supported with van and nice hotel accommodations.

Retreats and workshops are held at their small hotel, Fuentes de Lucia, in the mountains of northern Spain.

For additional information, visit them at:

www.spanishsteps.com
www.spanishstepsretreats.com

Totally Spain is an established and bonded Spain Travel Specialist based in Cantabria in Northern Spain. They specialise in quality customised travel throughout Spain. For the Camino de Santiago, they provide bespoke trips for Individuals and Groups that cater to each clients specific needs with regards to itinerary, trip duration, pace, transfers including baggage, professional guides, support vehicles, quality accommodation and more. Past clients include Walkers, Cyclists, Bikers, Coach Groups and Motorists. With Totally Spain you can do THE WAY in whatever way suits you.

www.totallyspain.com
email: **info@totallyspain.com**
Tel: UK 0709-229-6272 0871-6660214   SPAIN +34-942-637358   USA 561-828-0238

Walk the Camino.com

A specialist organiser of walks and tours on the Camino de Santiago; we do all the planning work so you can enjoy a stress free time on the Camino. We can arrange your travel within Spain, as well as a bag transfer on the Way. We've over ten years' expertise on the Camino serving customers from all over the world and tailoring walks from one day to one hundred days in length. WalkTheCamino takes the time to understand your requirements and creates a personalised itinerary designed specifically around your needs, interests and walking ability. WalkTheCamino offers both independent and guided walks along the Camino for all walking abilities, from the most scenic sections of the 'Camino Francés' to the quiet 'Vía de La Plata'. Our fully supported tours include luggage transfers, Credential and 24 hours assistance. Accommodation along the way includes hand-picked traditional and luxury hotels, inns and country houses chosen for their charm and personal level of service.
Tel: +44 141 956 1569 www.walkthecamino.com info@walkthecamino.com

Other tour companies

Outdoor Travel Pty Ltd
www.outdoortravel.com.au email
info@outdoortravel.com.au

Walkers' World
www.walkersworld.com
info@teacherstravel.com

Camino de Santiago Reservas
www.caminodesantiagoreservas.com
info@caminodesantiagoreservas.com

Hotels that accept pets
The majority of Spanish hotels, restaurants and bars are hostile to pets but there is a website that lists hotels that will accept dogs.
www.aceptanperros.com

Camino websites that list alternative accommodation

www.jakobusfreunde-paderborn.eu/Download.html
www.Caminosantiago.com : Click on Lodging
www.mundicamino.com : Links to hotels on all routes

Chapter 4

WALKING STAGES AND ITINERARIES

Most Camino guide books suggest 32 to 35 day walking stages. If you start in St Jean Pied de Port, this means walking an average of 23km to 25km per day. Some days will be shorter than the average but even on a 35 stage itinerary (such as the one suggested in John Brierley's guide to the Camino Frances) it will be necessary to walk longer distances on some days - 3 days of 27kms, 3 days of 29km and 3 days of over 30km. Most people are more comfortable walking shorter distances than these.

With this in mind, I have prepared four walking itineraries based on:

>   10km to 15km per day
>   15km – 20km per day
>   20km – 25km per day
>   5km – 8km per day on the last 100km to Santiago for not so able pilgrims

The number of days required to walk the full distance from St Jean Pied de Port will increase with each itinerary but you can adjust these by skipping a few stages, or combining them where the terrain is flat and easy. Some of the paths on the Camino Frances are fairly challenging. Others, mostly in and out of larger cities, are long hard slogs on pavements through light industrial and urban residential areas. Some paths run next to busy highways where you have cars and trucks rumbling alongside you for a couple of days. I have made suggestions where to avoid these sections by taking transport off the trail.

Daily Stages

The four Daily Stage itineraries offered here have been compiled, with permission, using the Camino Planner **website www.godesalco.com/plan** (See Appendix 3 on how to use this website to compile your own itinerary.)

Suggested accommodations are budget, based on personal experience or recommendations. There are often many other places to stay especially in large villages and towns. Places change, go under new management, or close down. Where places don't have websites, I have included a telephone number or email address. Many places now have FACEBOOK pages so search for them there if they don't have websites. Please check each place before making your reservation and if any places have closed, please let me know via my book website, www.sylvianilsenbooks.weebly.com

Notes for these Itineraries

1. If you start in St Jean add 2 days and 25km to these itineraries.

2. All places listed in BOLD are private albergues that also have single and/or double rooms as well as dormitories. Staying in these will give you the 'best of both' experiences. You'll be in your own room but can also interact with other pilgrims you want to.

3. Some hotels, pensiones etc will give a discount to a pilgrim on presentation of a credencial.

4. If you dislike steep, rocky downhill paths, before leaving Pamplona arrange for a taxi to collect you from the top of the Alto de Perdón - 13.7 km from Pamplona. The view from up there is spectacular but the path down is a real ankle snapper, steep and strewn with rocks and river boulders.

    On Itinerary 1, the taxi can take you 10 km down the hill to Obanos. On the other two itineraries, you could be dropped at Zariquiegui or Uterga

    Accommodation in Obanos:
    Casa Villazon 2: www.casavillazon.com
    Or, at Casa Rural Raichu : **www.casaraichu.com**

5. It is a long, 8km slog through the residential and commercial district of Burgos from Villafria into the centre of town! I recommend you take a bus into town.

6. Walking into Leon past car graveyards and factories is not pleasant. When you get to the outskirts of the town, call for a taxi to collect you and take you to your booked accommodation or get on a bus. (Taxi numbers: Appendix 5)

7. For about 1.5 days, the walk out of Leon is on an asphalt track next to a busy highway with very little shade and heavy trucks bearing down on you in both directions. Rather get a bus to Hospital d'Orbigo and start walking from there. Buses leave almost every hour from the bus station in Leon, heading for Astorga. Ask the driver to let you off at Hospital de Orbigo.

8. The steep, rock and shale track from El Acebo down to Molinaseca is one of the most challenging on the Camino Frances. The alternate route is to walk on the road which is the same distance but much kinder on the legs! It is not a busy road but remember to face the on-coming traffic and walk in single file.

9. The climb up to O Cebreiro (1300m) on the rock and shale path can be gruelling, especially in bad weather. If it is misty or raining, rather walk on the road. The same applies to the path down to Triacastela.

10. You start your 100 km walk to Santiago from Sarria. From now on you must get two stamps in your credencial each day.

Itinerary 1: 10km to 15km daily stages

Summary

Total Distance:	± 684 km
Shortest stage:	8 km Molinaseca to Ponferrada
Longest stage:	17.2 km A Rua
Stages:	59 (from Roncesvalles) 57 walking stages
Daily average:	12.42 km

Stage	Daily (km)	Total (km)	Suggested Accommodation
Roncesvalles			Casa Sabina www.casasabina.es Or La Posada www.laposadaderoncesvalles.com
1 Viscarret	11.6	11.6	La Posada Nueva www.laposadanueva.net
2 **Zubiri**	**10.2**	**21.8**	**El Palo de Avellano. www.elpalodeavellano.com**
3 Picnic site - *Taxi to Pamplona*	12.4	34.2	Pension Sarasate (Booking.com) http://pensionsarasate.es
4 Pamplona to Alto de Perdon Taxi to Obanos	13.7	47.9	Casa Raichu www.casaraichu.com
5 Obanos - Cirauqui	10.5	58.4	Hostel Maralotx Tel: 678 635208

Stage		Daily (km)	Total (km)	Suggested Accommodation
6	Estella	13.9	72.3	Hostal Cristina Tel: 948 550 450
7	Villamayor de Monjardín	9	81.3	Casa Rural www.casaruralmontedeio.com
8	Los Arcos	12.1	93.4	Pension Mavi www.pensionmavi.es
9	**Torres del Río**	**7.6**	**101**	**La Pata de la Oca** **reservas@alberguelapatadelaoca.com**
10	Viana	10.3	111.3	Pension San Pedro www.pensionsanpedro.com
11	Logroño	9.9	121.2	La Redonda Or Booking.com www.casaconencanto.net
12	**Navarrete**	**12.5**	**133.7**	**EAlburgue el Cantaro** **www.alberguelcantaro.com**
13	Nájera	16.2	149.9	Hostal Hispano www.hostalhispanonajera.com
14	Cirueña (FR 200 m)	15.2	165.1	Casa Victoria www.casavictoriarural.com
15	Grañón	13.4	178.5	1km from Grañón www.irj.es/ermita_carrasquedo_ en_granon

Stage	Daily (km)	Total (km)	Suggested Accommodation
16 Villamayor del Río	10.9	189.4	La Aldea Encantada www.laaldeaencantada.es
17 Villafranca de Montes de Oca	16.4	205.8	La Alpargatería http://tinyurl.com/a9dl2fd
18 San Juan de Ortega	12	217.8	La Henera www.sanjuandeortega.es
19 Villaria	14.7	232.5	Hostel Iruñako www.irunako.es
20 Bus to Burgos			Abba Burgos (or Booking.com) www.abbaburgoshotel.com/en
21 Rabé de las Calzadas	12.6	245.1	Hotel Rural Deobrigula www.escapadarural.com
22 Hornillos del Camino	7.7	252.8	Casa Rural Sol da Sol www.desolasoln3.es
23 **Hontanas**	**10.5**	**263.3**	**Albergue Puntido www.puntido.com**
24 Castrojeriz	9.5	272.8	La Posada www.laposadadecastrojeriz.es
25 Itero de la Vega	10.9	283.7	Hostal Puente Fitero www.iterodelavega.com/turismo

Suggested Accommodation

Stage	Daily (km)	Total (km)	Suggested Accommodation
26 Frómista	13.9	297.6	Hotel San Martin www.hotelsanmartin.es
27 Villalcázar de Sirga	12.9	310.5	Hostal Infant Leonor www.hostal-infantaleonor.com
28 Carrión de los Condes	5.7	316.2	Hostal la Corte www.hostallacorte.com
29 Calzadilla de la Cueza	16.9	333.1	Hostal Camino Real www.turwl.com/caminoreal/index.html
30 Moratinos	12.3	345.4	Hostal Moratinos www.hostalmoratinos.es
31 Sahagun	10.5	355.9	Hostal Escarcha www.hostalescarcha.com
32 **El Burgo Ranero**	**13**	**368.9**	**Hostel La Laguna** **Tel: 987 33 00 94**
33 **Reliegos**	**12.9**	**381.8**	**Albergue La Parada** **www.alberguelaparada.com**
34 Puente Villarente	12	393.8	Hostal Montaña www.hostalrestaurantelamontana.es
35 Leon	16	409.8	San Martin (or Booking.com) www.sanmartinhostales.es

Stage	Daily (km)	Total (km)	Suggested Accommodation
36 Bus to Hospital de Orbigo			El Paso Honroso www.elpasohonroso.com
37 Astorga	15	424.8	Hotel Astur Plaza www.hotelasturplaza.es
38 Rabanal	16	440.8	El Refugio www.hostalelrefugio.es
39 El Acebo	15	455.8	La Rosa de lagua www.larosadelagua.com
40 Molinaseca	9	464.8	Casa Reloj antonio.rojo@pfizer.com
41 Ponferrada	8	472.8	Hostel Los Templarios www.hotellostemplarios.es
42 Cacabelos	15.1	487.9	Hostal la Gallega www.hostalgallega.com
43 Trabadelo	12.7	500.6	El Puente Peregrinos http://elpuenteperegrino.blogspot.com
44 Vega de Valcarce	11.3	511.9	Pension Fernandez purrusaldalove@hotmail.com
45 O Cebreiro	11.8	523.7	Hotel San Giraldo de Aurillac Tel: 982 367 125

Stage	Daily (km)	Total (km)	Suggested Accommodation
46 Fonfría	11.9	535.6	Albergue A Reboleria www.albergueareboleira.blogspot.com
47 Triacastela	8.9	544.5	Complexo Xacobeo www.complexoxacobeo.com
48 Samos	9.9	554.4	Hostal Victoria Samos www.hostalvictoriasamos.es
49 Sarria	14.7	569.1	Hotel Alfonso IX (Or Booking.com) http://sarriahotelalfonsoix.com
50 Morgade	12.1	581.2	Casa Morgade www.casamorgade.com
51 Portomarín	10.4	591.6	**Albergue Ultreia!** **www.ultreiaportomarin.com**
52 Ventas de Narón	13.2	604.8	**Albergue O Cruciero** **http://albergueocruceiro.blogspot.com**
53 Palas de Rei	11.6	616.4	Pension Bar Plaza www.pensionbarplaza.es/situacion.php
54 Melide	14.6	631	Hotel Carlos www.hc96.com
55 Arzúa	14.3	645.3	Pension Arcano www.pensionarcano

Stage	Daily (km)	Total (km)	Suggested Accommodation
56 Salceda	11	656.3	Pousada de Salceda www.pousadadesalceda.com
56 Salceda	11	656.3	Pousada de Salceda www.pousadadesalceda.com
57 A Rua	17.2	662.5	Hotel O Pino www.hotelopino.com
58 Lavacolla	11.5	674	Hostal Ruta Jacobea www.rjacobea.com
59 Santiago de Compostela	10.2	684.2	Hospederia San Martin Pinario www.sanmartinpinario.eu

Itinerary 2: 15km to 20km daily stages itinerary

Summary
Longest stage: Villalcázar de Sirga - Calzadilla de la Cueza: 22.6 km
Shortest stage: Sarria - Morgade: 12.1 km
Total distance: 748.7 km
Stages: 42
Daily average: 17.8 km per walking day

Stage	Daily	Total (km)	Suggested Accommodation (km)
Roncesvalles			Casa Sabina www.casasabina.es Or the Posada www.laposadaderoncesvalles.com
1 Visacarett	11.6	11.6	La Posada Nueva www.laposadanueva.net
2 Larrasoana	16	27.6	Pension el Camino www.sangalo.net/web4.htm
3 Pamplona	14.9	42.5	Pension Sarasate http://pensionsarasate.es
4 Obanos	21.2	63.7	Casa Raichu www.casaraichu.com
5 **Lorca**	**15.9**	**79.6**	**La Bodega del Camino www.labodegadelcamino.com**
6 Villamayor de Monjardín	17.5	97.1	Casa Rural www.casaruralmontedeio.com
7 **Torres del Río**	**19.7**	**116.8**	**La Plata del a Orca reservas@alberguelapatadelaoca.com**
8 Logroño	20.2	137	La Redonda www.casaconencanto.net
9 Sotes	16	153	Casa el Colorao www.casaruralelcolorao.com

Stage	Daily (km)	Total (km)	Suggested Accommodation
10 Azofra	18.5	171.5	Real Casa de las Amas (4-star) www.realcasonadelasamas.com/localizacion.html
11 Santo Domingo de la Calzada	15.1	186.6	Hotel el Corregidor www.hotelelcorregidor.com
12 Villamayor del Río	18.6	205.2	La Aldea Encantada www.laaldeaencantada.es
13 Villafranca de Montes de Oca	16.4	221.6	La Henera www.sanjuandeortega.es
14 Atapuerca	18.2	239.8	Casa Rural Casarrota http://www.casarrota.com
15 Burgos	19.5	259.3	Booking.com or Abba Burgos www.abbaburgoshotel.com/en
16 Hornillos del Camino	20.3	279.6	Casa Rural Sol da Sol www.desolasoln3.es
17 Castrojeriz	20	299.6	Puerta de la Monte www.puertadelmonte.es
18 Boadilla del Camino	19	318.6	Casa en el Camino Tel: 979 810 284
19 Villalcázar de Sirga	18.7	337.3	Hostal Infant Leonor www.hostal-infantaleonor.com

Stage	Daily (km)	Total (km)	Suggested Accommodation
20 Calzadilla de la Cueza	22.6	359.9	Hostal Camino Real www.turwl.com/caminoreal/index.html
21 Sahagún	21.8	381.7	Hostal Escarcha www.hostalescarcha.com
22 **El Burgo Ranero**	**17.7**	**399.4**	**Hostel La Laguna Tel: 987 33 00 94**
23 Mansilla de las Mulas	19.1	418.5	La Pension de Blanca www.lapensiondeblanca.com
24 León	18.1	436.6	San Martin (or Booking.com) www.sanmartinhostales.es
25 Villadangos del Páramo	20.1	456.7	Hotel Avenida1-II http://hotelavenidaiii.com/
26 **Vilares Orbigo**	**14.2**	**470.9**	**Alerbgue Villares www.alberguevillaresdeorbigo.com**
27 Astorga	13.9	484.8	Hotel Astur Plaza www.hotelasturplaza.es
28 Rabanal	20.2	505	Posada Tesin posadaeltesin@hotmail.com
29 El Acebo	16.6	525.1	La Rosa de lagua www.larosadelagua.com

Stage	Daily (km)	Total (km)	Suggested Accommodation
30 Ponferrada	16.1	537.7	Hostel Los Templarios www.hotellostemplarios.es
31 Villafranca del Bierzo	**22.3**	**560**	**Albergue Piedra** **www.alberguedelapiedra.com**
32 Las Herrerías	20.4	580.4	Paradiso del Bierzo www.paraisodelbierzo.com
33 Fonfría	20.1	600.5	Casa Nunez Tel: 982-161335
34 Samos	18.8	619.3	Pensión Domus Itineris www.domusitineris.com
35 Sarria	14.7	634	Pension Escalinata www.pensionescalinata.es
36 Morgade	12.1	646.1	Casa Morgade Tel: 982 531 250 www.casamorgade.com
37 Gonzar	**18.5**	**664.6**	**Casa Garcia** **Tel: 982 157 842**
38 Palas de Rei	16.7	681.3	Pension Bar Plaza www.pensionbarplaza.es
39 Melide	14.6	695.9	Hotel Carlos www.hc96.com

Stage	Daily (km)	Total (km)	Suggested Accommodation
40 Arzúa	14.3	710.2	Pension Arcano www.pensionarcano.com
41 O Pedrouzo (FR 500 m)	18.5	728.7	Pension Maribel www.pensionmaribel.com
42 Santiago de Compostela	20	748.7	Hospederia San Martin Pinario www.sanmartinpinario.eu

Itinerary 3: 20 km to 25 km daily stages itinerary

Summary

Longest stage: Palas de Rei - Ribadiso da Baixo: 25.8 km.
Shortest stage: Lédigos - Sahagún: 15.6 km.
Total distance: 748.7 km.
Stages: 35
Daily average: 21.4 km per walking day.

Roncesvalles	0	0	Casa Sabina www.casasabina.es Or the Posada www.laposadaderoncesvalles.com
1 Zubiri	21.8	21.8	Pension Amets pensionamets@gmail.com

Stage	Daily (km)	Total (km)	Suggested Accommodation
2 Pamplona	20.7	42.5	Hostal Hemingway www.hostelhemingway.com
3 **Puente la Reina**	**23.5**	**66**	**Jakue Hotel** **http://www.jakue.com**
4 Estella	22.1	88.1	Pension San Andres Tel: 948554158
5 **Los Arcos**	**21.1**	**109.2**	**Casa de la Abuela** **www.casadelaabuela.com**
6 Viana	17.9	127.1	Casa Armendariz www.casaarmendariz.es
7 **Navarrete**	**22.4**	**149.5**	**El Alburgue el Cantaro** **www.albergueelcantaro.com**
8 Nájera	16.2	165.7	Hostal Hispano www.hostalhispanonajera.com
9 Santo Domingo de la Calzada	20.9	186.6	Hostal R Pedro 1 www.hostalpedroprimero.es
10 Belorado	23.4	210	Hotel Jacobeo www.hoteljacobeo.net
11 San Juan de Ortega	23.6	233.6	La Henera www.sanjuandeortega.es

Stage	Daily (km)	Total (km)	Suggested Accommodation
12 Burgos	25.7	259.3	Booking.com or Hostal Lar www.hostallar.es
13 Hornillos del Camino	20.3	279.6	Casa Rural Sol da Sol www.desolasoln3.es
14 Castrojeriz	20	299.6	La Posada www.laposadadecastrojeriz.es
15 Boadilla del Camino	19	318.6	Casa en el Camino Tel: 979 810 284
16 Carrión de los Condes	24.4	343	Hostal La Corte* www.hostallacorte.com
17 Terradillos de los Templarios	**23.1**	**366.1**	**Albergue los Templarios www.alberguelostemplarios.com**
18 Sahagún	15.6	381.7	Hostal la Codorniz www.hostallacodorniz.com
19 El Burgo Ranero	17.7	399.4	Hostel La Laguna Tel: 987 33 00 94
20 Mansilla de las Mulas	19.1	418.5	Hostal San Martin www.hostalsanmartin.es
21 León	18.1	436.6	Booking.com or www.hotelsleon.net

Stage	Daily (km)	Total (km)	Suggested Accommodation
22 Villadangos	24.8	461.4	Hotel Avenidal-II http://hotelavenidaiii.com
23 San Justa de la Vega	24.5	485.9	Hostal Juli www.hostaljuli.com
24 Rabanal del Camino	**23.8**	**509.7**	**Posada Tesin posadaeltesin@hotmail.com**
25 Molinaseca	24.8	529.8	Casa el Palacio www.casaelpalacio.com
26 Cacabelos	23	552.8	Hotel Moncloa de San Lazaro www.moncloadesanlazaro.com
27 Vega de Valcarce	24	576.8	Pension Fernandez purrusaldalove@hotmail.com
28 Fonfría	23.7	600.5	Albergue A Reboleria www.albergueareboleira.blogspot.com
29 Samos	18.8	619.3	Hostal Victoria Samos www.hostalvictoriasamos.es
30 Barbadelo	**19**	**638.3**	**Casa de Carmen www.acasadecarmen.com**
31 Portomarín	18.2	656.5	Hotel Villa Jardin www.hotelvillajardin.com

Stage	Daily (km)	Total (km)	Suggested Accommodation
32 Palas de Rei	24.8	681.3	Pension Palas www.pensionpalas.es
33 Ribadiso da Baixo	25.8	707.1	Casa Vaamonde http://prvaamonde.comoj.com
34 Rúa	20.9	728	Hotel O Pino www.hotelopino.com
35 Santiago de Compostela	20.7	748.7	Hospederia San Martin Pinario www.sanmartinpinario.eu

Itinerary 4: 5km to 8km, 17 daily stages from 100km to Santiago

his itinerary is for the not-so-able or disabled walking pilgrim and is based on the 100
m amaWalkers Camino SLOW CAMINO walk from Barbadelo to Santiago undertaken
1 17 days.
Courtesy amamwalkersCamino.com)

Accommodation is booked in small hotels, pensiones, hostales and private albergues for two or three nights so that you don't have to unpack and pack every day. Local taxis are used to shuttle you from the trail to the hotel, and back to the trail the next day.

NB: Taxis charge ± €1.5 per km. The approximate cost of taxi services in the schedule is based on 4 people sharing.

Sarria: Miguel Angel 667397348 or Andres 608081184:
Portomarin - David 639628262:
Palas do Rei - Daniel 608920354, Oscar 655025606:
Melide: Albert 608581206, Chucho 669578087, Kiko 606673749
Santiago: Victor, 608983990

Notes for this itinerary:

There are often detours available around the more difficult sections of the Camino paths and alternatives to follow the road. Although these are small country roads, please face oncoming traffic, walk in single file and take care when crossing the road.

1. **From Mercado de Serra to Peruscallo:** The section deviates onto a dirt track which leads to a stream. One crosses by means of several large stepping stones in the river. You can avoid this difficult stretch by continuing on the N-540.

2. **Peruscallo to Casal:** The section starts on a steep, gravel path. You can use the N-540 to reach Casal and Brea.

3. **The path deteriorates after Morgade** to loose gravel, stones and steep slopes. You can use the N-540 until Ferrerios. Thereafter the path is paved and presents no problems.

4. **From Villacha to Portomarin** it is safer to use the road as the rocky path is steep and uneven.

5. **Leaving Portomarin,** you can remain on the road to avoid the steep climb through the forest.

6. **From Toxibo to Palas de Rei** the alternative route is on the C-135. This section is generally suitable for people with disabilities, excepting for a short stretch between Gonzo and Hospital da Cruz which is steep and narrow.

7. **From Casanova,** the path consists of three distinct sections. The first is smooth, compacted stone and presents no difficulties. The second section of about 300m is loose stone, with a very steep ascent which might make it inaccessible for severely disabled walkers. The third section is paved and the gradient is very mild.

8. **From Campanilla to Castaneda** the path is reasonably easy. If you need to use an alternate route, the LU-633 is not far off the path.

9. **From Leboreiro to Furelos** (4km): The path, which leads to the N-547 and then back onto the trail, is not very difficult although there are several ascents and descents.

10. **From Furelos to Melide** (1.9km): The difficulty could be negotiating the sidewalks and busy intersections in the town.

11. The path shadows the N-547 (which can be used by wheelchair users instead of the path) all the way to Arzua. There are steep descents and ascents in and out of Ribadiso.

12. **From Arzua to Arca** there are no insurmountable difficulties.

13. **From Arca to Monte de Gozo:** The road is accessible until leaving Monte de Gozo. 500m beyond the large complex, one must use a flight of steps to reach the pavement below. To avoid the steps it is possible to use to the road for about 80m.From here on you are in the outskirts of the city with a long, hard slog on pavements and road crossings to the Cathedral.

Note:

The healthcare system in Spain is good, and local hospitals in Santiago provide accident and emergency services.

Nationals of EU member states who can produce a European Health Insurance Card (EHIC) are eligible for temporary medical care services at the same facilities that care for Spanish citizens.

Several other countries follow the European community rules, including Iceland, Liechtenstein, Norway and Switzerland. Citizens of these countries are also eligible for the same healthcare benefits as Spanish nationals.

In addition, Spain has reciprocal healthcare arrangements with Andorra, Brazil, Chile, Ecuador, Paraguay and Peru.

Nationals of all other countries will need to pay for medical services when received and are advised to take out comprehensive healthcare cover in advance of their visit.

112 is the Europe-wide emergency number. It works even if you have no money in a pre-paid mobile phone or even if your supplier has no network. It works 24/7 365 days – and the operators speak many languages.

092 is the number for the Police

062 is the number for the Guardia Civil

061 is the number for the ambulance

080 is the number for the Fire Brigade.

17-day, 5km to 8km stages

Places to walk to each day (5km to 8km)	Km per day		Overnight Place & Hotel	Taxi transfers: From – To AM and PM	Km by taxi	Total km	Taxi €1.2 per km
First night in Sarria			Sarria Escalinata				
(Taxi to Barbadelo) Walk to Casal	6.2	6.2	Sarria Escalinata	AM: Sarria to Barbadelo PM: Casal to Sarria	4.5 10.7	15.2	€5.5 €18.5
Walk to Mercadoiro	6.3	12.5	Portomarin Ultreia!	AM: Sarria to Casal PM: Mercadoiro to Portomarin	10.7 5.7	16.4	€20
Walk to Portomarin	5.7	18.2	Portomarin Ultreia!	AM: Portomarin to Mercadoiro PM: No taxi	5.7	5.7	€7
Walk to Gonzar	8.1	26.3	Portomarin Ultreia!	AM: No Taxi PM: Gonzar to Portomarin	8.1	8.1	€10
Walk to A Prebisa	7.1	33.4	Palas de Rei Pension Plaza	AM: Portomarin to Gonzar PM: A Prebisa to Palas de Rei	8.1 9.6	17.7	€21
Walk to Brea	6.8	40.2	Palas de Rei Pension Plaza	AM: Palas de Rei to Prebisa PM: Brea to Palas de Rei	9.6 2.8	10.8	€13

Places to walk to each day (5km to 8km)	Km per day		Overnight Place & Hotel	Taxi transfers: From – To AM and PM	Km by taxi	Total km	Taxi €1.2 per km
Walk to San Xulian	6.3	40.2	Palas de Rei Pension Plaza	AM: Palas de Rei to Prebisa PM: Brea to Palais de Rei	9.6 2.8	10.8	€13
Walk to San Xulian	6.3	46.5	Palas de Rei Pension Plaza	AM: Palas de Rei to Brea PM: San Xulian Palas de Rei	2.8 3.5	6.3	€7.5
Walk to Leboreiro	5.8	52.3	Melide Hotel Carlos	AM: Palas de Rei to San Xulian PM: Leboreiro to Melide	3.5 5.3	8.8	€10.5
Walk to Melide	5.3		Melide Hotel Carlos	AM: Melide –Leborerio	5.3	5.3	€6.5
Walk to Boente	5.9	63.5	Melide Hotel Carlos	No taxi PM: Boente to Melide	5.9	5.9	€7
Walk to Ribadiso Carretera	6.2	69.7	Arzua Pen/Arcano	AM: Melide to Boente PM: Ribadiso Arzua	5.9 2.2	8.1	€9
Walk to Pereiriña	7.2	76.9	Arzua Pen/Arcano	AM: Arzua to Ribadiso PM: Pereiriña to Arzua	2.2 5	7.2	€9
Walk to Salceda	6	82.9	Arca -Pension Maribel	AM: Arzua to Pereiriña PM: Salceda to Arca	5 7.4	12.4	€15

Places to walk to each day (5km to 8km)	Km per day	Km per day	Overnight Place & Hotel	Taxi transfers: From – To AM and PM	Km by taxi	Total km	Taxi €1.2 per km
Walk to Arca	6	8.29	Arca -Pension Maribel	AM: Arca to Salceda PM: No taxi	7.4	7.5	€9
Walk to San Paio	7.7	98.1	Monte de Gozo	AM: No taxi PM: San Paio-Monte de Gozo	7.9	7.9	€9.50
Walk to Monte de Gozo	7.8	106	Monte de Gozo	AM: Monte de Gozo-San Paio PM. No Taxi	7.7	7.9	€9.25
Walk to Santiago	4.4	110	Santiago	No Taxi Luggage Transfer	4.6	4.6	€5.50
						±160km	±€200

- When you get to Santiago you can visit the pilgrim's office in Rua do Vilar to collect your Compostela.
- Attend the mid-day pilgrims' mass the following day when the numbers of pilgrims from different countries are called out.
- Climb up the steps to the main altar to hug the saint.
- Descend the steps under the altar to the crypt to view the reliquary casket that holds his remains.
- Sit in the square and welcome pilgrims you met along the way as they arrive.

Chapter 5

Detours on the Camino Frances
(from Your Camino)

When planning to walk the Camino Frances, allow a few extra days for detours from the Camino path. There are many interesting, historical places just a few kilometres off the actual path that are not on the modern Camino but which probably were a part of alternate trails in the Middle Ages. Some will add a few kilometres to your walk, others you can reach by bus or take a tour.

Ibaneta Pass

If you start in Roncesvalles, try to get there early enough to take a 3 km walk up to the 1 300 m Ibaneta Pass and look into France from the top. The famous monastery and hospice of San Salvador once stood here. There is a modern chapel here dedicated to Charlemagne and a monument to Roland. This is where the Route Napoleon and the Val Carlos Route join.

Roncesvalles

Many pilgrims start at Roncesvalles (or stagger in late from St Jean Pied de Port!), but because they arrive on the evening bus, they don't have time to explore this historic monastery complex. Try to get there the day before, or take a taxi from Pamplona (share the fare with other pilgrims) so that you have time to visit the cloisters and the museum with its extraordinary reliquaries and other artifacts. Scan the church walls for mason signs; visit the old walls of the original hospice opposite the church and the monastery ossuary that is said to hold the remains of Charlemagne's soldiers.

Eunate

From Muruzabel and Obanos, about 3 km off the Camino path, is the octagonal church of Santa María de Eunate. Built around 1170 it has been associated with the Knights Templar and excavations close by have revealed numbers of graves with scallop shells suggesting that it could have been a funerary church. The walls have many mason signs that you will see all along the Camino.

Clavijo

18 km south-west of Logroño is the ruined castle of Clavijo, reputedly the site where Santiago first appeared on a white horse at a battle to help the Christian soldiers against Moor armies. You can take a taxi there or walk there and back in two days.

San Millán de la Cogalla

14 km south-west of Azofra are the magnificent monasteries of Suso and Yuso, the first built between the 5th and 6th centuries and the Yuso around the 16th century.

Atapuerca

Book a guided tour to the fascinating archaeological site which lies within a military zone about 40 km from the village. Atapuerca is one of Europe's most important archaeological sites. It was declared a World Heritage Site in 2001. (No private visits allowed.) info@atapuerca.es

Santo Domingo de Silos

Take a bus from Burgos to the monastery where the Gregorian chants were made famous a few years ago. (The trip itself is an experience, along narrow winding roads, through stunning, rock-face scenery.) The cloisters are unique and the pharmacy museum is worth a visit.
The bus leaves Burgos at 17h30 and returns at 08h30 the next day, not leaving enough time to see the village, hear the chanting and visit the museum so plan on spending at least two nights.
www.hotelsantodomingodesilos.com

Castrojeriz

climb the hill and visit the ruins of the castle Mirador with spectacular views of the alleys below and horizons that stretch forever! Visit the Convent of Santa Clara about km south of the village – a closed order – where you can buy biscuits and other baked goodies by passing your money through a revolving serving hatch.

Las Medulas

About 20 km from Ponferrada, the fantastical landscape of the Medulas used to be the most important gold mine in the Roman Empire. Las Médulas landscape is listed by UNESCO as a World Heritage Site.

Vega de Valcarce

You will see the Castle Sarracin squatting on the high hill to your left on the way to O Cebreiro. Originally built in the 9th century, it was owned by the lords of Sarracin who also owned 35 small towns in the area. This 14th century castle was one of eight castles owned by the Marques de Villafranca. A round trip of about 45 minutes will reward you with extensive views and an impressive ruin that has sheer cliffs on three sides.

Eirexe

A 6 km detour to the recently restored, spectacular monastery of San Salvador at Vilar das Donas.

Finisterre and Muxia

About 90 km west of Santiago is the small fishing village of Fistera or Finisterre, known as The End of The World in medieval times. The bus takes about 2.5 hours or you can walk there in three to five days and earn the Fisterrana certificate.

25 km north of Fistera and the final destination of Santiago pilgrims, is Muxia where legend has it that the Virgin Mary appeared to an evangelic apostle. The Celtic stones near the church are said to be remains of the Virgin Mary's stone boat.

Padron

South-west of Santiago you can visit the church of Santiago which contains the 'Padron' stone under the altar. This is the stone where Saint James' disciples tied their stone boat when they came ashore with his body which they had brought from the Holy Land.

Appendix 1

'Camino Lingo" ACCOMMODATION

Checking in

hotel	**el hotel**	*oh-tel*
pension	**la pensión**	*pen-see-on*
hostal	**el hostal**	*oh-stal*
rural house	**la casa rural**	*ca-sa ru-ral*
rooms	**las habitaciones**	*ah-bee-ta-thee-oh-nes*
camping	**el camping**	*cam-peen*

I have a reservation	**tengo una reservación**	
	ten-goh una reh-ser-va-thee-on	

from...to...	**desde...a...**	*des-deh .. ah...*
the date	**la fecha**	*feh-cha*

Do you have a..?	**¿hay?**	*ai*

a single room	**una habitación individual**	
	ah-bee-ta-thee-on een-dee-vee-doo-al	

a double room	**una habitación matrimonial**	
	ah-bee-ta-thee-on mah-tree-moh-nee-al	

a twin-bed room	**una habitación con dos camas**	
	ah-bee-ta-thee-on con dos ca-mas	

a triple room	**una habitación con tres camas**	
	ah-bee-ta-thee-on con tres ca-mas	

a quad room	**una habitación con cuatro camas**	
	ah-bee-ta-thee-on con kwat-roh ca-mas	

With	**con ....**	*con*

en suite bathroom	**un baño**	*ba-nios*
a shower	**una ducha**	*du-cha*
a shared bathroom	**baño compartido**	*ba-nios com-par-tee-doh*

One/two .. nights	**una noche… dos noches**	
	oo-na noh-cheh.. dos noh-ches	
How much is it?	**¿cuánto es?**	*kwan-toh es*
How much is it?	**¿cuánto es?**	*kwan-toh es*
Check out time?	**¿la hora de salida?**	*oh-ra deh sa-lee-da*
Please write it down	**escríbalo por favor**	*es-cree-ba-lo por favor*
Can I pay by credit card?	**¿Puedo pagar con tarjeta de crédito?**	
	Pweh-doh pa-gar con tar-kheh-ta deh creh-dee-toh	

Appendix 2

Packing lists

Ladies

ITEMS	NO	In the pack	Wear	Carry
2L Backpack	1	600		
Backpack Liner	1	127		
Sea to Summit day pack	1	71		
Sleeping bag liner	1	192		
Small Pillow (optional)	1	144		
Staff	1			300
Hi Tec Shoes	1		728	
Gaiters & spare shoe laces	1		83	
Croc sandals	1	182		
Hiking socks	3	202	101	
Short sleeve shirts	2	95	95	
Long sleeve top	1	177		
Long sleeve fleece with zip	1		168	
Shorts - quick dry	2	96	98	
2 Long lightweight trousers	1	133		
Parachute jacket	1	162		
Backpack Raincoat - ALTUS	1	460		
Panties	3	76	38	
Bras	2	33	33	
Hat & peak	1		94	
Sun Screen	2	64		27
Waist Bag/small purse	1			182
Glasses & Case	1	12		
Camera/Case & lanyard	1			273
Head lamp	1	98		
Credencial	1			20
Maps & Guide	1	111		70
Money	1			65
Spanish Dictionary	1			48
Notebook & pen	1			27
Passport	1			42
Toiletries and bag	1	169		
Camp towel	1	150		
1/2 toilet roll	1	38		
Laundry Bag, 8 pegs, soap	1	157		
5 mesh laundry bags	1	100		
Cup, immersion heater, plug	1	247		
Plasters, Arnica, Tea tree oil	1	298		
First Aid items	1	244		
2 X 500ml bottles	2			65
Plate & cutlery	1	73		
Sitting Plastic	1	30		
		4674	**1438**	**1119**

Extra with water & food in backpack

Mens

Backpack
Sleeping sack
Hydration bag 1.5l
Poncho
Gaiters
Gloves polypro
Knit cap
Tilley hat
Bandana
Crocs

LS shirt-wicking
Travel LS shirt
SS shirt-Lowe Alpine
T-shirt polypro
GoLite wind jacket
Fleece-polypro
Breathable jacket
Convertible pants
Belt

Under pants
Wool/poly socks
Polypro liner socks
Handkerchief
Stuff sacks
Dry bag
Clothes line-elastic

Ear plugs
towel
Universal charger
Plug converter
USB card reader
Swiss Army knife
Trekking poles
Pen
Guide book
Money belt
Wallet
Passport
Credential

Ivory bar soap
tooth brush
tooth paste
Camp soap laundry

Silicone ointment
Compeed plasters
Sunblock
Toilet paper
Bandaids
Antiacid
Prescriptions
Ibuprofen

First aid kit
Hand sanitizer
Hand wipes
Nail clipper
Cup
KFS titanium

Drivers license
Credit card
Debit card
Phone list
Eyeglass case

Watch
Flashlight
Whistle
Camera/chip
Cell phone/SIM chip

Appendix 3

Camino Planner

You can use this website to plan your daily stages from Roncesvalles. It will give you profile maps, albergues, sunrise and sunset and lunar illumination times. www.godesalco.com/plan.

* How to use the **www.godesalco.com/plan** website to plan your daily schedule:

- Once connected to the site click on English.

- Click on the route you are doing – Camino de Santiago for the Camino Frances.

- Click on the circle ◉ to the left of the town where you are starting, e.g.: Roncesvalles

- Scroll down to the town where you will finish, Santiago, and click on the right

- circle. ◉

- You can type your name in the space provided, then click on SEND THIS FORM.

- In the new page, the mileage between each village and town will be displayed.

- Click on each place where you would like to stay. If you are planning on walking 20km per day, click on the town closest to the 20km distance displayed to the left of the town. E.g.: Roncesvalles is ticked so click on Zubiri – 21,8km will be displayed. Then click on Pamplona and 20,5km will be displayed.

- Continue choosing your overnight stops until you have reached Santiago. Enter the dates of your pilgrimage in the space provided.

- Click on SEND THIS FORM and the next window will offer you different documents to download with your daily schedule, profile of the route etc.

- After downloading an option, click on the 'BACK" facility on the page to download another option. (If you click on the back option on the search engine you will lose the page.)

Appendix 4

Trains and buses

Trains

RENFE www.renfe.es
The Spanish national train system

RENFE AVE
The Spanish high speed train system

RENFE CERCANÍAS
The Spanish local train system

RENFE REGIONALES
The Spanish medium distance trains

FEVE www.feve.es
A train system serving northern Spain

EUSKOTREN www.euskotren
A train system serving Basque Country

To book a train online visit:
www.rumbo.es

France

SNCF www.sncf.com
The French national train system

TGV www.tgv.com
The French high speed train system

TER www.ter-sncf.com
The French local train system

TER AQUITAINE www.ter-sncf.com/aquitaine
The train for Bayonne to Saint Jean Pied de Port

SNCF TRANSILIEN www.translien/com
The trains for Ile-de-France (Paris & vicinity)

RATP http://www.ratp.info/touristes
Metro, RER and trains for Ile-de-France (Paris & vicinity)

SEAT61.com
Train systems throughout the world

Buses

Bus companies serving the Spanish Caminos

There are numerous bus companies servicing the Camino routes in Spain, many are comfortable, clean and affordable. They will help you get to the beginning of your Camino and they are also useful if you are pushed for time, get injured or feel like taking a few side trips.

After days and weeks of simple walking however, it can feel a little strange and the sense of speed can be a little frightening!

ALSA Bus

Alsa buses run throughout Spain but more importantly they also run services along the length of eight Spanish Camino routes allowing you to travel back to the town or city you flew into at the start of your trip. Alsa buses are modern and comfortable and their website is full of useful resources and handy interactive maps.

Follow this link to their St James way bus services.
www.alsa.es
The Camino routes they cover are;

Camino Frances
Camino Norte
Camino Primitivo
Camino Portuguese
Camino Vasque
Camino Aragones
Camino Sanabres
Camino Vie de la Plata

They also serve Porto in Portugal

Continental – Auto
http://www.movelia.es/transicion_continental/venta.htm#

Avanza bus
Their site is in Spanish and English and covers mostly the east coast of the country but also Madrid, Galicia and even Torreblanca in Portugal
www.avanzabus.com/web/default.aspx

Monbus
A company running buses from Santiago to Sarria and Ferrol. (Sarria being a popular starting point for people wanting to walk the final 100km of the Camino Frances). This company also serve La Coruna from Santiago.
www.monbus.es

Empresa Freire
A company established nearly 100 years ago runs from Santiago to the airport, Arzua, Melide and Lugo
www.empresafreire.com/html/ingles/seccion0.htm

Conda
Running from Madrid and San Sebastian to Pamplona
www.condasa.com/colabora.php?idi=eng

La Burundesa
Buses linking Pamplona to San Sebastian, Logroño, Bilbao and Vitoria
www.laburundesa.com

Transportes Pesa
Buses linking Biarritz, San Sebastian, Bilbao and Bayonne
www.pesa.net

Autocares Artieda
Buses running from Pamplona to Roncesvalles with a rather confusing website!
www.autocaresartieda.com/

Mancobus
This company run from Jaca to Somport but at present have no functioning website. Details may be available locally.

Alosa
This company run from Pamplona to Jaca but also Barcelona and Puente la Reina.
www.alosa.es

Vibasa
Buses running from Barcelona to Pamplona
www.vibasa.es

La Sepulvedana
Very modern bus company, originating from Madrid with a clear, informative website in several languages including Japanese.
www.lasepulvedana.es

Camino Frances bus companies

The following section details the bus companies that serve towns and cities along the Camino Frances in Spain.

Laburundesa serve the Camino towns of Irun, Pamplona, Logroño, Santo Domingo and Belorado as well as the Northern coastline. However, do take a look at their route maps as their buses do not follow a logical routing.
For example, to travel from Irun to Logroño you must first use La Burundesa to Pamplona and then another company, La Estellesa to get to Logroño.
www.laburundesa.com

La Estellesa serves Pamplona, Estella, Los Arcos and Logroño
www.laestellesa.com

Grupo Jimenez serves the region of Rioja through Logroño and Zaragoza to Burgos
www.grupo-jimenez.com/rutas.html

Logroño Buses
Here is a list of all of the bus companies and routes serving Logroño that you may find useful.

Alsa Bus	Gijón - Oviedo - León - Logroño
Automóviles Soto y Alonso	Burgos - Briviesca - Logroño
Continental Auto	Vitoria - Logroño
Herederos de Juan Gurrea	Azagra - Lodosa - Mendavia - Logroño
La Estellesa	San Sebastián - Logroño
La Unión Alavesa	Bilbao - Logroño
Viacar (ALSA)	Santander - Logroño
Vibasa	Vigo - Pontevedra – Orense - Logroño
Zamorana de transportes	Valladolid - Logroño

Logroño to Najera and beyond
www.riojanosenlared.com/AUTOBUSES.htm

Aupsa serve many locations along the Camino Frances including Ponferrada, Villafranca de Bierzo, Foncebadon in the mountains, Manjarin and La cruz de Ferro.
www.aupsa.es/rutasbierzo.html

Buses from Santiago de Compostella

Triacastela
To travel between these two destinations, first you must use Empresa Freire buses to Lugo then Monbus to Triacastela.
www.empresafreire.com/html/ingles/seccion0.htm
www.monbus.es

Finisterre
www.monbus.es
Timetable: Santiago to Fisterra - 9am - 10am - 1pm - 7pm
Returning: 8h20 - 11h45 - 16h45 (they've dropped the 14h45 and 7pm bus)

Muxia
Two buses daily (one early morning, one mid afternoon) link Santiago to Muxia and the journey takes 2 hours again from the main bus station.
www.tussa.org

Camino Aragones
Buses serving the Camino Aragones from Jaca to Somport
Daily services operated by Jaca Turismo
www.jaca.es/turismo_busjaca.php

Buses from Madrid

There are two main bus stations in Madrid - so the station you'll need depends on where you are going.
The main station is Méndez Alvaro (also known as Estación del Sur) which mainly serves buses to the south, east and north-west. If you cannot find a destination at the other stations, it will probably be covered by this one. The station is located in the sout of the capital.

The other is Avenida de America in the north-east of the city. It has its own Metro station and the airport bus goes straight there as well.
Sevilla
Cádiz
Córodoba
Huelva
Jerez de la Frontera
www.estaciondeautobuses.com/

The north station - Estación de Avenida de América serves;
Bilbao
San Sebastián
Vitoria
Burgos
Santander
Pamplona
Logroño
Soria
Guadalajara
Toledo
Granada

Madrid's metro map - click on "Plano"
www.metromadrid.es/

Travelling from Madrid to Salamanca or Zamora
Use Auto-Res buses.
www.venta.avanzabus.com

Other useful transport links

Public transport in Madrid
A comprehensive site with a few handy interactive planning tools
www.ctm-madrid.es/

Movelia – Spanish bus search engine
www.movelia.es/

us company in France

his company serves the area of Bayonne, Hendaye and Biarritz useful if you plan to
tart from St Jean Pied de Port and arrive by air. Their site is in French.
vww.transdev-atcrb.com/index.php?rub=horairesettarifs

Bus lines from Santiago de Compostela

ALSA
Tel: 902 42 22 42
www.alsa.es

ALSA ROUTES

Santiago – Germany
Santiago – Belgium and Holland
Santiago – France and Switzerland
Santiago – Porto
Santiago - Porto - Lisboa
Santiago - Zamora - Salamanca
Santiago - Zamora - Salamanca - Mérida - Sevilla - Algeciras
Santiago - Madrid
Santiago - Burgos - Zaragoza - Barcelona
Santiago - Ponferrada - Astorga - León - Valladolid
Santiago - Asturias
Santiago - Asturias - Santander - Bilbao - San Sebastián - Irún
Santiago - Ponferrada - Palencia - Burgos - Vitoria - Bilbao

ARRIVA Noroeste
902 27 74 82
www.arriva.es

Santiago - Curtis
Santiago - Curtis - Vilalba
Santiago - Curtis - Vilalba - Mondoñedo - Burela / Ribadeo
Santiago - As Pontes - Viveiro
Santiago - Padrón - Araño - Boiro - Ribeira
Santiago - Padrón - Rianxo - Boiro - Ribeira
Santiago - Boiro - Ribeira - Aguiño (por AP-9 e vía rápida)
Santiago - Ferrol (por AP-9 e Guísamo)
Santiago - Ferrol (por AP-9 e Fene)
Santiago - Ferrol (por AP-9 e Pontedeume)
Santiago - Ordes - Betanzos - Miño - Pontedeume - Ferrol

Castromil / Monbus
Tel: 902 29 29 00
http://www.monbus.es

Routes

Santiago - A Coruña (por AP-9)
Santiago - Sigüeiro - Ordes - A Coruña
Santiago - Pontevedra - Vigo (por AP-9)
Santiago - Padrón - Caldas de Reis - Pontevedra - Vigo
Santiago - Ferrol (por AP-9 e Pontedeume)
Santiago - Ordes - Betanzos
Santiago - Noia
Santiago - Noia - Muros
Santiago - Muros - Cee - Fisterra
Santiago - Noia - Muros - Cee - Fisterra
Santiago - Lalín - Ourense (por AP-53)
Santiago - Silleda - Lalín - Ourense
Santiago - Silleda - Lalín - Ourense - Verín
Santiago - Silleda - Lalín - Chantada - Monforte
Santiago - Silleda - Lalín - Chantada - Monforte - A Rúa - O Barco
Santiago - Cacheiras - Cuntis - Moraña
Santiago - Vilagarcía - Cambados - O Grove - A Toxa
Santiago - Vilagarcía - Vilanova - Cambados - O Grove - A Toxa
Santiago - Vilagarcía - Cambados - Sanxenxo - O Grove - A Toxa

Empresa Freire
Tel: 981 58 81 11
www.empresafreire.com

Routes

Santiago - Lugo (via AP-9 e A-6)
Santiago - Airport - Arca - Arzúa - Melide - Palas de Rei – Lugo, Dr. Teixeiro - estación de autobuses – airport
Santiago - aeroporto - Arca - Arzúa
Santiago - aeroporto - Arca - Arzúa - Sobrado
Santiago - Ferreiros

Hermanos Ferrín
Tel: 981 87 36 43
Routes

Santiago - Bertamiráns - Negreira
Santiago - Bertamiráns - Negreira - Muxía
Santiago - Tapia - Piñeiro
Santiago - A Baña - Santa Comba
Santiago - Picaraña
Santiago - Reborido
Santiago - Casalonga

Appendix 5

TAXIS

Navarra

Luzaide/Valcarlos
Andoni Urolategi
Tel: 948 79 02 18 / 636 19 14 2

Carlos Mateo (Only luggage)
Tel: 948 79 00 43 / 676 27 45 50

Auritz/Burguete
Juanjo
Tel: 670 61 61 90

Aurizberri/Espinal
Francisco Igoa
Tel: 948 79 03 86 / 649 72 59 51

Garralda
Angel M. Loperena
Tel: 948 76 40 58 / 609 41 14 49

Mezkiritz
Pedro Ernaga
Tel: 609 43 62 26

Zubiri
Fermín Ventana
948 30 40 67 / 609 44 70 58
Miguel Larragueta
Tel: 948 30 40 06
(no bicycles)

Pamplona
Teletaxi
948 351 335/Reserve by email
info@taxipamplona.com

Puente la Reina
Taxi Castellanos
Tel: 610 69 88 17 / 619 44 99 12

Estella/Lizarra

Luis Manuel	Tel: 636 699 872
Maribel	Tel: 636 765 939
Taxi Estella	Tel: 679 634 101
Taxi Luis	Tel: 617 463 865
Servi Taxi	Tel: 608 329 551
Central taxis	Tel: 948 555 001

Los Arcos
Taxi Los Arcos

Tel: 650 9652 50 / 639 40 45 38

Viana
Raúl Jubera   Tel: 663 921 888

La Rioja
Logroño
Unitaxi: Tel: 941 50 50 50
Logroño taxi   Tel: 696 985 435
www.logrotaxi.com

Tramos   Rioja Tel: 941 10 14 10
www.tramos.es

Taxi 24-hours   Tel: 678 53 28 93

Calahorra
Taxis   Tel: 941 13 00 16

Cervera del Rio Alhama
Taxis 941 19 89 91

Hormilleja Abalonstaxi: Tel: 619,164,913
www.abalonstaxi.com

Lardero
Taxis   Tel: 941 43 65 65

Euro Taxi Lardero: Tel: 667 84 73 84
www.eurotaxilardero.es
Enrique Taxi: Tel: 678 602 729

Nájera

Ignacio Pascal	Tel: 608 67 73 28
Najera Taxi	Tel: 647 44 31 16
Guillermo	Tel: 680 96 91 44
Mauricio Gomez	Tel: 941 36 14 75

Navarrete
Tel: 656,684,950
axinavarrete@gmail.com
Navarette Taxi services
Tel: 941 101 410/630 975 528
www.taxinavarrete.com

BURGOS

Burgos Taxi Associations (186 vehicles).
www.abutaxi.com
abutaxi@yahoo.es more

www.radiotaxiburgos.es
radiotaxiburgos@gmail.com more

Palencia
Tel: 696 443 722
www.radiotaxipalencia.com

Castrojeriz
Z & Z Autocares Tel: 979 72 00 16
www.autocareszyz.es
info@autocareszyz.es

Fromista
Elisa Vallejera Tel: 979810079
Casa Vallejera Tel: 979810079

Carrion de los Condes
Luis Angel Tel: 650 451 540
www.taxiluisangel.com

Sahagun
Taxi Sahagun Tel: 659563390
www.taxisahagun.com mavi46@gmail.com

Leon
Taxi Leon Tel: 659 92 92 91
info@taxispaco.es
http://taxileon.blogspot.com

Leon Radio Taxis
Tel: 987 26 14 15

Astorga
Radio Taxis
http://www.radiotaxileon.com
Taxi Astorga
http://www.taxiastorga.com/

Ponferrada
Radio Taxi
D. Raúl Jato   Tel: 987 087 087
www.radiotaxiponferrada.com
central@centraltaxiasturias.com

Villafranca del Bierzo
Jesús López   Tel: 987 540 305 / 679 972 797
Pedro Cao   Tel: 654 701 957
Roberto   Tel: 696 074 780
Jose López   Tel: 636486062
Dositeo   Tel: 679 440 956

O Cebreiro
Rubio   Tel: 626 58 77 96
Pepines   Tel: 982 36 71 65
Fermin   Tel: 609 67 43 03

Tricastela
Elva Campo Veiga 659 893 588
Fernandez Pardo, Aurita 982 548 037

Sarria
Miguel Angel   Tel: 667397348
Andres   Tel: 608081184

Portomarin
David 639628262:

Palas do Rei
Daniel   Tel: 608920354
Oscar   Tel: 655025606

Melide
Albert   Tel: 608581206
Chucho   Tel: 669578087
Kiko   Tel: 606673749

Santiago
Victor   Tel: 608983990
Radio Taxi   Tel: 981 56 92 92
Euro 88   Tel: 619 90 30 24
http://eurotaxisantiagodecompostela.blogspot.com/

Taxi Galicia   Tel: 611 00 00 00
www.taxigalicia.com

Books published by LightFoot Guides

All LightFoot Publications are also available in ebook and kindle and can be ordered directly from www.pilgrimagepublications.com

LightFoot Guides provide the following:
Instruction sheet/s comprising:
Detailed directions corresponding to GPS way point numbers on the maps
Distance (in metres) between each way point Verification Point - additional verification of current position
Compass direction Maps comprising:
A visual representation of the route with way point numbers and adjacent details
Altitude Profile for the section
Icons indicating places to stay, monuments etc.

Each volume contains detailed routing instructions, route and town schematics and listings of accommodation and services. Purchasers of the books are entitled to receive GPS Way Point data and periodic route updates for the area covered.

Lightfoot Guides to the Via Francigena 2013

The complete 2013 LightFoot Guide to the via Francigena consists of 4 books:

1. Canterbury to Besançon
2. Besançon to Vercelli
3. Vercelli to Rome
4. Companion to the Via Francigena

In the 2013 edition the authors continue to use the official route in Italy, as approved and signed by the Italian Minister of Culture, but also offer additional opportunities where it is too challenging for one or more groups.

LightFoot Guide to the via Domitia - Arles to Vercelli

Even with the wealth of historical data available to us today, we can only offer an

approximate version of yesterday's reality and we claim to do nothing more in this book. The route described runs roughly parallel with a section of the via Domitia between Arles and Montgenévre (a large portion of the original route having been subsumed by the A51), continues along a variety of roads and tracks that together form a modern-day branch of the via Francigena and rejoins the official main route (to Rome) in Vercelli.

The LightFoot Companion to the via Domitia is an optional partner to the guide, providing the additional historical and cultural information that will enhance your experience of the via Domitia and via Francigena

The LightFoot Guide to the Three Saints' Way

The name, Three Saint's Way, has been created by the authors of the LightFoot guide, but is based on the three saints associated with this pilgrimage: St Swithin, St Michael and St James. Far from being a single route, it is in fact a collection of intersecting routes:

The Millenium Footpath Trail starting in Winchester and ending in Portsmouth, England.
The Chemin Anglais to **Mont St Michel** and the **Plantagenet Way to St Jean d'Angely**, where it intersects with the St James Way (starting from Paris).

LightFoot Guide to Foraging
Heiko Vermeulen

"Nowadays if I look at a meadow I think lunch."
A guide to over 130 of the most common edible and medicinal plants in Western Europe, aimed at the long-distance or casual hiker along the main pilgrim routes through Western Europe. The author has had some 40 years of experience in foraging and though a Dutchman by birth, has been at home all over Europe including Germany, Ireland, England and for the last 8 years in Italy along the Via Francigena pilgrim route, where he feeds his family as a subsistence farmer, cultivating a small piece of Ligurian hillside along permaculture principles, and by gathering food from the wild.